GROUP FACILITATION

THEORIES AND MODELS FOR PRACTICE

John Heron

Kogan Page Ltd, London
Nichols Publishing Company, New Jersey

First published in 1993

Kogan Page Limited
120 Pentonville Road
London N1 9JN

© John Heron, 1993

British Library Cataloguing in Publication Data
A CIP record for this book is available from the British Library.

ISBN (UK) 0 7494 0970 3

Published in the United States of America by Nichols Publishing, PO Box 331, East Brunswick, New Jersey 08816.
A CIP record for this book is available from the Library of Congress.

ISBN (US) 0-89397-385-8

Typeset by the author
Printed and bound in Great Britain by
Biddles Ltd, Guildford and King's Lynn

Contents

Chapter 8. Structural change

Foreword

This book is a sequel to *The Facilitators' Handbook*, published by Kogan Page in 1989. That work presents a model of facilitation as the use of three forms of power applied to six dimensions of the learning process. These three forms I call the decision-modes of hierarchy, co-operation and autonomy: deciding unilaterally for learners, deciding in consultation with them, and delegating decisions to them. The six dimensions are: course planning, issues of meaning, confronting resistance, issues of feeling, structuring the immediate learning experience, valuing personhood.

On this foundation, the present work offers further theories and models for the facilitator of experiential learning groups. Chapter 1 introduces the model of facilitator authority as tutelary, political and charismatic, in relation to both autonomy and holism in learning. Tutelary authority is a new concept and is fully fleshed out in practical terms. Political authority means aware use, on different levels, of the three decision-modes of hierarchy, co-operation and autonomy: the analysis here deepens that of *The Facilitators' Handbook* and shows how such use can empower students and effect the integration of holistic and autonomous learning through course design.

Chapter 2 is entirely devoted to the notion of charismatic authority - personal presence and power. It gives an account of the theoretical model I use in charismatic training for facilitators, together with training exercises which have been field-tested with participants from many different professional fields. This chapter substantially develops a theme which was mentioned in only a sentence or two in *The Facilitators' Handbook*.

Chapter 3 opens with several basic distinctions in the field of whole person learning, and then concentrates on holistic learning applied to some specific subject or skill. It examines the experiential learning cycle in relation to views of the whole person, and outlines the model of personhood from my book *Feeling and Personhood* (1992). This model is the basis for a new version of the experiential learning cycle in terms of primary and secondary cycles, and of open ego and whole person learning. There is an analysis of superlearning, and of the issue of teacher-managed and student-managed cycles. The chapter ends with an account of the many elements that can fall within a holistic, multi-stranded approach to learning that does not use formal cycles.

Chapter 4 is devoted to the idea of learning how to be a whole person. It presents a systems theory model of the whole person as a nexus of internal and external relations including the intrapersonal, the interpersonal, the cultural, the ecological and the transplanetary ('transpersonal' in current usage) domains. This framework is used to define the whole person as a change agent of a comprehensive kind; to identify a wide range of whole person learning agendas and the different locations in which they occur; to develop the importance of action inquiry - the experiential learning cycle in living - and of the self-generating learning culture it seeks to establish; and to define the basic set of values and human rights involved.

Chapter 5 takes up a basic theme from Chapter 4, that whole person learning occurs in a wide range of different areas of life, and works it through in detail in one location: the workplace. The current revolution of organizational forms is briefly reviewed. The six dimensions and three decision-modes of *The Facilitators' Handbook* are now transposed and reinterpreted to illuminate a model of the manager as the facilitator of personal development in the workplace. This yields 18 basic management options, applied to enhance personal development and action inquiry in the organization through an increase of self and peer determination and decentralization in all aspects of work, balanced by appropriate federal hierarchy.

The context for this application is a theory of workteam dynamics, developed in terms of the following factors: the structure of the team; the tasks of the team; the motives of its members; critical issues to do with the team's organizational and social contexts; ideology; the authority of the manager; and the vision of the manager. The analysis ends with a holocratic set of values to illumine the facilitation of personal development in the workplace. This chapter shows how the model put forward in *The Facilitators' Handbook* for the training centre, can be transposed to the workplace, thus bringing out the overlap between facilitation and management.

A basic point made in Chapter 5 is that management as the facilitation of personal development in the workplace means the generation of increased self and peer determination within the team. Chapter 6 shows how any facilitator/management trainer can promote autonomy on the meaning dimension of work by enabling people to run their own peer review audit groups. Such groups give meaning to their job by a form of self-directed quality control of performance, through systematic action inquiry. Peer review audit is a radical kind of peer supervision whereby a small group of people in the same profession come together in regular meetings to develop and apply standards of professional competence. This chapter gives an account of all the stages of the method, together with notes on facilitation and training issues at each stage, and with illustrative comments from actual audit histories. Only one page was devoted to peer review audit in *The Facilitators' Handbook* .

Chapter 7 continues the theme of self and peer determination, autonomous development and action inquiry in groups, by describing a wide range of peer supervision strategies of a less complex and demanding form than peer review audit, but all having proved their merit. Details of the sequential stages for each of these are given, together with notes for the facilitator introducing it in a training programme. The later part of the chapter looks at peer support groups that are not exclusively focussed on work-related issues and extend to personal life. And the same format is used of detailing the stages, together with notes for facilitators. The theme of learning how to be a whole person launched in Chapter 4 is here unfolded in terms of the emergence of self and peer development groups for working and living, in which autonomy and holism become self-generating. Facilitation is only involved in the launching.

The peer supervision and peer support groups considered in Chapters 6 and 7 will have as their outcome transformations of individual behaviour which can change the face-to-face quality of life in the surrounding culture, without addressing its structure as such. Chapter 8, the final one, looks at personal development as individual and collective action inquiry involved with structural change of the culture. It reviews three different theoretical approaches to social structures, distinguishes between liberation within and liberation from the human condition, and between opposing oppression and fulfilling rights. It concludes with the different group options available for working explicitly on the transformation of social structures, and with the issues of concern to which the facilitator can alert any such group.

John Heron
Murrays Bay, New Zealand
January, 1993

Acknowledgements

Staff development training is a valuable crucible for refining theories and models for practice. I am grateful to Shona Todd of the Centre for Professional Development, Auckland Institute of Technology, for organizing a comprehensive series of workshops in New Zealand between November 1991 and March 1992; to the ASB Grants Committee for their financial support; and to the many participants for their creative involvement, which has provided the immediate stimulus for the writing of this book.

Recent discussions with several friends and colleagues have been influential. David Boud and Sue Knights provided congenial hospitality during a week's visit to the University of Technology in Sydney, and focussed my mind on several issues raised in this book. Grethe Hooper-Hansen has been instructive about suggestive-accelerative learning, considered in Chapter 3. A day of shared vision and analysis with Russell Withers in Mairangi Bay, Auckland, provided a backdrop for the ideas put forward in Chapters 4 and 8. A meeting with William Torbert gave me a deeper appreciation of his notion of transforming power, referred to in Chapter 5. Peter Reason and John Mulligan gave helpful comment on an earlier version of the content of Chapter 5.

Chapter 1 is a revised and enlarged version of 'The Politics of Facilitation' paper presented at the University of Surrey Conference on *Empowerment through Experiential Learning* in 1991, and published in the book of conference papers by Kogan Page in 1992. Chapter 5 is a revised and enlarged version of Chapters 1 and 2 of *A Handbook for Leaders*, published in a limited edition by the Human Potential Resource Group, University of Surrey, 1990. Chapter 6 is a revised, enlarged and up-dated version of 'Self and Peer Assessment for Managers' which appeared in Boydell, T and Pedler, M (eds) *Management Self-Development*, London, Gower Press, 1982. I am grateful to the publishers concerned for their permission to print revision of this material here.

1. Authority, autonomy and holism

Three kinds of facilitator authority

The facilitator has three kinds of authority - tutelary, political and charismatic. Tutelary authority means that the facilitator has mastered some body of knowledge and skill, and appropriate procedures for passing it on; can communicate effectively to learners through the written and spoken word and other presentations; can care competently for learners and be a guardian of their needs and interests.

In the old days this would have been limited to mastery of some field of knowledge, and simply called cognitive authority, but nowadays a purely cognitive account of such authority is too restrictive. The word 'tutelary' has the connotation not only of tuition in a body of knowledge, but also of care and guardianship and so it is closer to what is needed. Even so it will need to be given an expanded definition; and this I do in a later section.

Political authority means that facilitators take decisions that affect the whole programme of learning. It involves the exercise of educational decision-making with respect to the content, methods and timing of learning. Charismatic authority means that facilitators influence learners and the learning process by virtue of their presence, style and manner, that is, through their personal delivery of tutelary and political authority. Charismatic facilitators empower people directly by the impact of their way of being and behaving.

Authority and authoritarianism

We need here to distinguish a benign, luminous and truly educative authority from a punitive, indoctrinating and intimidating authority. Genuine authority proceeds from those who are flourishing from their own inner resources and can thereby enable other people to flower in the same way. It manifests as the facilitative ability to empower. So charismatic authority as I defined this in the preceding section is really central to it, interacting with tutelary and political authority.

Oppressive authority is rigid authoritarianism and proceeds from people who are denying some of their basic inner resources and can only use a model of overcontrol in trying to educate others. It manifests as the manipulative power to dominate. It has been the bane of education at all levels. Traditional teaching, still strongly with us, is beset by authoritarianism. It runs the different kinds of authority into each other.

Traditional confusion of three kinds of authority

Old-style teaching confuses the three kinds of authority in the crudest possible way. It assumes that because teachers have cognitive authority - as repositories of knowledge - they should therefore exercise total political authority in a *directive* way, making all educational decisions *for* their students. And then it assumes that because they have to direct everything that students do, they should exercise their charismatic authority as controlling power, that is, as disciplinarians and judges, meting out punishments to the disobedient, and judging the learners' conformity by acts of unilateral assessment.

Thus the traditional teacher decides what students shall learn, when and how they shall learn it and whether they have learnt it; and presides over this regime with a forbidding authoritarian charisma. Student autonomy is relegated to in-the-head following of many long lectures, to answering questions or asking them, and to doing homework on prescribed reading, writing or practical tasks.

Need for authority

The challenge of all teaching is to integrate a genuine authority in the facilitator with the autonomy of the learner. But why have any kind of educational authority, however benign? The obvious answer is so that knowledge and skills can be passed on. Otherwise everyone has to learn everything from experiential scratch - which would be the *reductio ad absurdum* of experiential learning theory. Herein lies the tension, between passing-on on the one hand, and the self-generated nature of personal learning on the other.

Learning as autonomous and holistic

Learning by its nature is autonomous: it is constituted by understanding and skill, retention and practice, interest and commitment. There is an obvious connection between learning and the first four of these, for they are what we mean by it: to learn is to come to understand something or to acquire a skill, either of which is retained by practice or rehearsal. And these are all necessarily self-generated: no-one else can do your understanding or retention or practice for you. But there is also a very close connection between learning and interest and commitment. We learn what interests us, that is, what is useful or intrinsically worthwhile or both; and because it interests us we are committed to stay the course until we have learnt it. Both interest and commitment are also necessarily self-generated: they are negated or distorted by any attempt to impose them.

But while the immediate process of learning is self-generated, does it follow that a whole programme of learning is necessarily self-directed? Up to a point it clearly does: interest and commitment of any authentic sort call for some degree of self-directed planning in how to fulfil learning goals (Boud, 1988). They cannot be sustained in a programme that is entirely directed by others, without degenerating into compulsive prudence - conforming to the system in order to survive as effectively as possible. There are two other arguments in favour of self-direction in educational decision-making about the procedures of learning.

The first is to do with the end product of the educational process, namely educated professionals. What society rightly expects in such persons is that they can monitor and intelligently manage their competence while they are working (Schön, 1983), they can learn from work experience by reflecting on it, they can assess their work in retrospect when it is done, and they can keep their work up to date by being a self-directed life-long learner. All these interdependent skills of being self-monitoring, self-reflective, self-assessing and self-directing need to be acquired during the undergraduate learning process in setting learning objectives and planning learning programmes, through the use of the experiential learning cycle, and by participation in assessment (Heron, 1988a). If they are not, then we cast inadequately prepared professionals into the public arena.

The second argument is to do with rights. The doctrine of natural rights was first clearly formulated by Locke in the 17th century, and has been on the march ever since. Now it is invoked in terms of human rights, which point to those moral principles that apply to people simply by virtue of their humanity and that transcend prevailing law, fiat or convention. One basic right is the right of people to participate in decisions being made about them. This has been applied historically in the political sphere and has been used and is still being used world-wide to press the case for democratic forms of government, in which people participate in political decision-making through their elected representatives.

However it is also a right calling for more widespread application, and it is this generalized extension which is still problematic and contentious for many people in our society who take for granted the political application. Growing children have a right to participate increasingly in parental decisions about their lives and welfare. Workers have a right to participate in managerial decisions that affect their work. Subjects in research experiments have a right to participate in researcher decisions that generate knowledge that purports to be about them. So too in the educational sphere, students in higher education - who are considered old enough to die for their country - have a right to participate in staff decisions that claim to educate them.

As well as being autonomous, learning is also necessarily holistic, that is, it involves the whole person, a being that is physical, perceptual, affective, cognitive (intellectual, imaginative, intuitive), conative (exercising the will), social and political, psychic and spiritual. It may involve the whole person negatively by the denial of some of these aspects and their exclusion from learning: in this case we get alienation, such as intellectual learning alienated from affective and imaginal learning, with the result that the repression of what is excluded distorts the learning of what is included. Alternatively the involvement is positive and all these dimensions are intentionally included in the learning process. But again, the unfolding and integration of multiple sides of the learner is a matter of self-development. A person blooms out of their own formative potential, in accordance with their own choices. The idea of someone who, after appropriate initiation, continues to live out an externally imposed, other-directed, programme of whole person development is a contradiction in terms.

An important supporting argument about holistic learning draws from general systems theory (von Bertalanffy, 1972; Laszlo, 1972), which, applied to psychology and learning, looks at people in terms of relation and integration. On this view the person is a system whose nature arises from the interactions of its parts: to educate such a person is to take account of the simultaneous and mutually interdependent interaction between his or her multiple aspects. Systems theory also asserts the primacy of self-organization in any dynamic system, and thus also underlines the arguments for autonomy in learning. In the later part of Chapter 3 I examine a systems account of holistic learning in some depth.

Paradox of facilitator authority

So the facilitator has to pass on some body of knowledge and skill - the content of learning - by a process of learning that affirms both the autonomy and wholeness of the learner. We thus get the paradox of facilitator authority exercised to generate free and rounded learning. This paradox is exacerbated in this era because it is a watershed time between two educational cultures. An authoritarian educational system, using oppressive forms of teacher authority, is still widespread; hence learners who emerge from it are conditioned to learn in ways that are relatively short on autonomy and holism. In a special sense they need leading into freedom and integration, when they enter another more liberated educational culture where these values are affirmed.

Authority as a means of initiation

The concept of *initiation* is, I think, the best one to illuminate this paradox. The facilitator's authority - tutelary, political, charismatic - is used to empower people through *rituals of entry* into their inner resources, their wellsprings of freedom and integration, the heritage of their personhood. This does mean a careful rethinking of what these three kinds of authority mean, especially the political kind. What happens to the facilitator's authority - tutelary, political and charismatic - in the model of teaching as initiation that empowers people with their autonomous and whole personhood? I will discuss each of these in turn, focussing most fully upon political authority. This is a very different concept of initiation to that originally evoked by R S Peters who used it to argue for the traditional model of unilateral staff control of the educational process (Peters, 1966).

Tutelary authority as initiation

Tutelary authority replaces the old idea of cognitive authority and is a much more sophisticated notion. I defined it in the opening section as mastery of some body of knowledge and skill and of appropriate methods for passing it on, effective communication to learners through the written and spoken word and other presentations, competent care for learners and guardianship of their needs and interests. By comparison with the old tradition, what is passed on and the passing on become much more comprehensive and varied. I will refer to these as subjects and procedures.

In relation to the subject, facilitators are not only intellectually competent in it, but also bring emotional, interpersonal, political, spiritual and other competences to bear upon their attitude to and presentation of it. They have a holistic grasp of the subject and can reveal it in a way that shows its interconnections with the all aspects of the person and with other interdependent subjects.

In relation to procedures, facilitators have a much more expanded repertoire than many traditional teachers in higher education, who have a limited range of methods and have received little or no training in the area. Being knowledgeable about diverse learning methods and skilled in their facilitation is essential for honouring autonomy and holism in learners. Here are some of the issues involved.

1. Open learning. There is a great emphasis on the provision of open learning materials: systems and packages of information and exercises - words and graphics - which are presented in a way that takes account of the self-pacing, self-monitoring learner.

2. Active learning. Much importance is given to the design and facilitation of holistic, participative methods - games, simulations, role plays, and a whole range of structured activities - which will involve learners in self-directing action and reflection, in affective and interpersonal transactions, in perceptual and imaginal processes. The facilitator uses the experiential learning cycle in various formats: this grounds learning in personal experience, and releases learning as reflection on that experience.

3. Real learning. Projects, field-work, placements and inquiry outside the classroom, case studies, problem-oriented learning, all these become vital aspects of the learning process, so that it is dynamically related to what is going on in the real world.

4. Peer learning. The autonomy of the learner needs the supportive context of other autonomous learners, hence the importance of the peer learning group for student co-operation in teaching and learning, experience and reflection, practice and feedback, problem-solving and decision-making, interpersonal process, self and peer assessment.

5. Multi-stranded curriculum. The curriculum is holistic and multi-stranded. This means several different and related things: the main subject on the curriculum is balanced by complementary minor subjects; each subject is talked about by the facilitator in a way that shows its interconnections with the whole person and with other interdependent subjects; the active learning methods used within a subject involve various aspects of the whole person, and may empower learning by evoking deep inner resources; the active learning methods used within a subject also bring out its impact on different aspects of the learner, and on its interdependence with other subjects; other activities in the classroom are not to do with the formal subject but to do with the self and others in ways that involve various aspects of the whole person.

6. Contract learning. The student is supported and helped to plan their own programme of learning and to participate in assessment of learning, by the use of collaborative contracts and collaborative assessment with the facilitator. This item overlaps with the facilitator's exercise of political authority, which I discuss below.

7. Resource consultancy. The amount of stand-up teaching becomes greatly reduced compared with the old approach: the facilitator becomes much more a resource and consultant, available to be called in when needed by the self-directing, active learner - to clarify, guide, discuss and support.

8. Guardianship. The facilitator cares for and watches over students as a guardian of their needs and interests, alerts them to unexplored possibilities, to new issues of excitement, interest and concern; and reminds them of issues discussed, of commitments made and contracts agreed. These eight items are illustrated in Figure 1.1.

The main tension in this list is focussed between items 5 and 6, holistic teaching and contract learning This especially applies where students have come from a very non-autonomous and non-holistic educational background, as is often the case with those who move from secondary to tertiary education. If these students start early on in a course to use learning contracts and thus to plan their own learning to a significant degree, then they are likely to do so in terms of the old familiar non-holistic learning methods they have brought with them. If, however, facilitators are going to initiate students into holistic methods, then the facilitators will have to plan a lot of the learning until students have internalized these methods and can manage them autonomously.

This tension between autonomy and holism in learning is, I believe, a major issue in the educational revolution that is afoot. In my view, it has not been sufficiently spotlighted in recent studies in experiential learning (Weil and McGill, 1989; Mulligan and Griffin, 1992). Many teachers are moving forward to use learning contracts and enhance student autonomy without considering whether the resultant learning process is holistic.

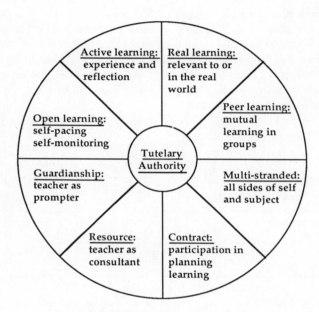

Figure 1.1 *Elements of tutelary authority*

Political authority as initiation: the three decision-modes

I defined political authority at the outset as the facilitator's exercise of educational decision-making with respect to the content, methods and timing of learning and teaching. A crucial shift is taking place in the use of this kind of authority in education, and so the concept of it needs to undergo a complete redefinition. I am not sure that the full implications of this have as yet been fully articulated and grasped. In a nutshell, the shift is from deciding in terms of just one decision-mode to *deciding which decision-mode to use*. The result is a vast increase in facilitator flexibility and enabling power. Let me explain.

By a 'decision-mode' I mean one of three basic ways of making educational decisions in relation to learners: you can make decisions for them, you can make decisions with them, or you can give them space to make decisions on their own, by themselves. These three decision-modes I will for convenience call, respectively, direction, negotiation and delegation. I have also called these hierarchy, co-operation and autonomy (Heron, 1989).

What the decisions are being taken about, centrally, are the basic elements of the learning process: learning objectives, the topics to be learnt, the pacing and progression of learning, the teaching and learning methods, the human and physical resources to be used, the criteria and methods of assessment.

If we combine topics with pacing and progression in the one item of the course programme, or timetable, then we have five main areas for educational decision-making: the objectives of learning, the programme of learning, the methods of learning, the resources (human and physical) for learning, and the assessment of learning. The three decision-modes and the five elements of the learning process are shown in Figure 1.2. The mention of level 2 in the figure title is explained in the next section.

	Objectives	Programme	Methods	Resources	Assessment
Direction: Facilitator alone					
Negotiation: Facilitator/Learners					
Delegation: Learners alone					

Figure 1.2 *Decision-modes for planning learning at level 2*

1. Direction. Direction, in the traditional full-blown form that is still used throughout most institutions of higher education, means that you exercise educational power unilaterally: you decide everything in the five areas *for* your students. You decide, without in any way consulting students, what they will learn, when they will learn it, how they will learn it and with what resources, and by unilateral assessment you decide whether they have learnt it. Students' performance with respect to objectives, the programme, methods, resources and assessment is entirely subordinate to your commands. Their self-direction can only be exercised in a minimal way within the complete framework of learning which you prescribe.

2. Negotiation. Full-blown negotiation means that you exercise educational power bilaterally: you decide everything *with* your students. Your decision-mode is co-operative. You take into account student self-direction, consult them about everything and seek to reach agreement in setting up mutually acceptable contracts about objectives, the programme, methods, resources and assessment. Assessment will be collaborative, involving a negotiation between students' self-assessments and your assessments of their work.

3. Delegation. Delegation means that you give space for the unilateral exercise of educational power by students themselves. In full-blown delegation, you have declared your own redundancy, and students are entirely self-determining with respect to their objectives, programme, methods, resources and assessment. Everything, including assessment, is self and peer determined in autonomous student groups.

Each of these decision-modes in its full-blown form as defined above is unacceptable as the exclusive basis for running any course in higher education. What is called for on an empowering course is that direction, negotiation and delegation are used in differing serial and concurrent ways as the course unfolds.

The old-style political authority of the teacher lacks any sophistication: it blindly applies the decision-mode of direction across the board of all educational decisions. The new facilitative political authority is more subtle and challenging: it means exercising liberating power by choosing the appropriate decision-mode - whether direction, negotiation or delegation - for these learners, at this stage of their learning, in respect of this or that aspect of the educational process. It means that you can influence the degree and the pacing of empowerment.

In *The Facilitators' Handbook* (Heron, 1989), these three decision-modes were considered in relation to six distinct dimensions of the learning process, which I called planning, meaning, confronting, feeling, structuring and valuing. In this chapter, I shall concentrate on their application to the planning dimension, where political authority is most fully exercised.

The four decision-mode levels

Now I want to refine this notion of political authority further, for there are four different levels at which these decision-modes can be applied. There is the main level, already mentioned, of planning the learning process in all its five aspects: learning objectives, the programme, the teaching and learning methods, the human and physical resources to be used, the criteria and methods of assessment.

As I have said, you can plan all this by yourself; or you can negotiate a plan with the learners; or the learners can put one together on their own. Below this, there is the ground-floor level of the immediate learning activity, what is going on in the classroom here and now: here too, you can manage it for the learners; or you can manage it co-operatively with the learners; or the learners can manage it on their own.

It is important to note that these two levels are quite distinct in the sense that different decision-modes can be used on them, and a lot of educational wisdom is involved in using these differences. Thus you can *directively* plan and structure a whole series of learning activities which in themselves involve a lot of *autonomous* management by the learners. This is a relevant combination for initiating people into deeply holistic forms of learning.

There is also a more abstruse third level, the level of deciding which decision-mode to use when planning. In other words, on level 3 you choose all by yourself a decision-mode for planning, or you negotiate with students in choosing a decision-mode for planning, or students all by themselves choose a decision-mode for planning. Many facilitators are probably not aware of level 3; that is, they are unawarely unilateral at this level without realizing there is a choice to be made between direction, negotiation and delegation.

Suppose you are going to negotiate with students at level 3. Then this means that before the course starts you take them aside and say: 'I want to invite you to take a conjoint decision with me as to whether I plan the course, you and I plan it co-operatively, or you plan it all by yourselves'. Such a consultation might result in a meta-plan in which you plan some parts of the course on your own, other parts are planned co-operatively, and yet further parts are planned by the students on their own.

There is a also fourth level for decision-mode use, but it is *necessarily and exclusively reserved for the directive mode*. This level is the final resting place of the facilitator's political authority. It is the level at which you decide which decision-mode to use at level 3, that is, which decision-mode to use in choosing a decision-mode for planning. It is at level 4 that you decide unilaterally, all on your own, whether at level 3 you will choose a decision-mode for planning by yourself, negotiate the choice with your students, or delegate to them the choice of a decision-mode for planning.

If at level 4 you choose negotiation at level 3, then you have unilaterally decided that you are going to ask your learners to negotiate with you in deciding whether you do the plannning, or you do it co-operatively with them, or they do it. As I say, this level 4 decision needs to be directive: you make it on your own.

It could be argued that you could negotiate or delegate at level 4, but then the decision to do either of those will have been taken directively at level 5. In other words there is an infinite regress of deferred decision-making, unless the series is closed by unilateral direction at some level, and level 4 is the highest possible level for rational closure. It is neurotic or mad to go beyond it. The four levels are shown in Figure 1.3. This figure provides a convenient anatomy of the exercise of facilitator power on any kind of educational course. The three decision-modes of direction, negotiation and delegation given in the figure refer to the options open to the facilitator at the different levels.

Level 4: Choosing a decision-mode to use in choosing a decision-mode in planning	Direction		
Level 3: Decision-mode to use in choosing a decision-mode for planning	Direction	Negotiation	Delegation
Level 2: Decision-mode used in planning learning activities	Direction	Negotiation	Delegation
Level 1: Decision-mode used in learning activity	Direction	Negotiation	Delegation

Figure 1.3 *Decision-mode levels*

Level 4 is a very abstruse level and many facilitators won't use it intentionally at all. Without noticing what they are doing, they will in effect decide directively at level 4 to decide directively at level 3 to use this, that or the other decision-mode in planning at level 2. If they are very, very unaware they will decide everything directively even at level 2, the level of planning, *without realizing they have other choices at that level*.

The simplest possible rendering of this figure is as follows. I decide at level 4 whether I, we or you decide at level 3 whether I, we or you plan at level 2 the programme of learning activities which will be managed by me, us or you at level 1.

Empowerment through mastery of decision-mode levels

I notice that facilitators tend to wilt rather when I go on about levels 3 and 4. Now it does require something like an extended state of consciousness to keep effectively alert at those levels. But I take the rather stringent view that until we have mastered those levels and know that we are using them and how we are using them - which usually means being directive at 3 as well as 4 and so unilaterally choosing decision-modes for level 2 - then we have not really taken charge of our power to empower our learners.

In other words, facilitators are, at crucial points in the most student-centred programmes, exercising a subtle kind of unilateral directive authority. They cannot abdicate from it at level 4, and will usually use it at level 3. Unless they are exercising it intentionally, and really know what they are up to, there is the ever present issue of unaware overcontrol or undercontrol of the empowering process.

Unilateral direction on principle at level 3

Many progressive facilitators are, even if they have not made this fully conscious to themselves, entirely directive at level 3 *on principle*. For example, they may believe strongly in a significant measure of student autonomy, such as student participation in programming their own learning and in assessing their own learning, both in conjunction with staff. They are committed to learning contracts and collaborative assessment as a matter of principle. And this principle is non-negotiable: they are not open to their learners negotiating them back into unilateral educational decisions. So at level 2 there is to be negotiated programming and assessment, but this use of negotiation at level 2 is itself non-negotiable at level 3.

Again, progressive facilitators may be committed to holism on principle, to educating many aspects of the person, so that both course content and learning methods are multi-dimensional. So they are non-negotiably directive at level 3 about being directive at level 2 with respect to holistic elements in programme design and in learning methods. Incidentally, facilitators who are committed at level 3 to both autonomy and holism face the challenge, at level 2, of using *negotiation* to affirm the autonomy, and *direction* to establish the holism. This is the creative tension between autonomy and holism to which I have already referred.

This business of being directive at level 3 on principle is entirely right and proper - so long as it is fully conscious and intentional. Authentic educators stand for certain inalienable and non-negotiable values to which they are deeply committed. If they do not stand for anything on principle and can be negotiated into *any* position, then they are not really educated and have no real authority of any kind, tutelary, political or charismatic. It is, ultimately and paradoxically, our non-negotiable values that empower people - or disempower them, depending on the values.

The importance of advertising non-negotiable values

What all this means is that facilitators' non-negotiable educational values - whether about autonomy or holism or both - which make them directive at level 3, should be consciously held, and above all clearly identified and made explicit in the course prospectus, and again at interview, so that the prospective learner can make a free and informed choice to join this particular community of value.

What the facilitators need to say loud and clear is: 'This is the kind of educational community we run, and we are committed in principle to students being autonomous and holistic in these various ways which we have specified. If this appeals to you, come and join us and explore this way of learning with us. If it is not what you want, we respect that, and invite you to look elsewhere for what you do want.'

This kind of pre-course clarity and openness is vital in principle, and especially in practice in a watershed culture where old and new models of education exist side by side and learners are moving between them. It is clearly immoral and not at all empowering to spring the new educational values on students after enrolment in their first weeks, when everything they have so far read or heard about the institution has led them to expect that it would deliver the old authoritarian values of unilateral direction of all learning by staff. If this surprise event happens to them, they have a valid moral case that the institution's implied contract to deliver traditional teaching has been broken. Many teachers who are enthusiastic to try new things make this mistake, and then fail to realize that they are not just meeting with some kind of psychological resistance to new methods, but even more so with a genuine moral grievance. Until students feel that their *moral* grievance is fully heard and honoured, there is not much chance that they will be able to work through their *psychological* resistance.

It may be that facilitators tend to be entirely directive at level 3 precisely because we live in this watershed culture between the old and the new educational values. If your learners are heavily conditioned by the old values, to negotiate with them or delegate to them at level 3 may simply mean that they unawarely press the claims of these old values. So it is better to decide directively at this level, make it clear in all the course publicity what your values are, and invite learners to join you if these values appeal to them, and to recommend that they do not join you if these values do not appeal. You need to offer an unequivocal contract to potential students about your mode of practice.

A full-blown level 3 course

However, there may come an era when the values of autonomy and holism are the norm in the educational culture. Then we have the prospect of a full-blown level 3 course in which students are included in negotiation at this level. So the course is advertised as one where the learners will be asked on arrival to co-operate with the staff in deciding whether the five main elements of the learning process will be planned by the staff, by staff and learners, or by the learners, or in different respects by each of these groups. Such a course does indeed sound empowering and full of potential learning.

Even now in professional development courses it can be realistic and grounded. I have used it on a course to train experienced GPs to become trainers of young hospital doctors entering general practice for the first time. To get a relevant course going I needed to agree, with the trainers coming to the course, on who should plan what: I certain things, they and I other things, they certain things.

The numerous options within level 2 courses

However let us now focus on level 2 and assume facilitators are directive at level 3, that is, they exercise their political authority unilaterally at level 3 to decide who at level 2 shall determine the many different aspects of the learning process: the facilitator alone, the facilitator in negotiation with the students, or self-directing students on their own. The facilitator as political authority in the new approach makes a selection from the table shown in Figure 1.2.

The column on the left shows the three basic decision-modes of direction, negotiation and delegation. The top row shows the five main areas of educational decision-making. The facilitator in setting up and running any course has enormous scope for making a large number of varied combinations of the decision-modes and the five areas. Different decision-modes can be used within one area - which can be broken up into several components - as well as between different areas. The combination used at the start will depend on the purposes of the course and the level of the learners; and may change as the course proceeds. There is also the possibility of opening up level 3 to learners at later stages of the course and inviting genuine negotiation or delegation at that level.

And it is important to remember, as I have already mentioned, that the decision-mode used in planning learning is quite distinct from the decision-modes used in managing the learning activities that are planned. For example, I can plan directively at level 2 a lot of autonomous learning activities at level 1. This may mean either that the activities have been structured by me and are to be autonomously managed by the students; or that both the structuring and the managing are to be done by the students.

Again, I can plan directively at level 2 negotiated field-work at level 1. Or a plan negotiated with students at level 2 may include directive methods such as stand-up teaching at level 1. And so on in a large number of possible combinations. The typical progressive course is unilaterally directive at level 3, may use any of the decision-modes at level 2, with much delegation - autonomous practice - at level 1.

The modern revolution in education and training has as yet scarcely got to grips with the flexible and imaginative use of this table, and with the many subtle and changing ways of distributing power between facilitator and learners throughout level 2, not to mention the different ways of distributing power as between levels 2 and 1, and within the learning activities on level 1 itself.

Examples of level 2 courses

Let me show this table at work in terms of two examples. First, consider a typical five-day management training course used by a major UK company today. The trainers specify the objectives of the course, design the programme, choose the methods and resources - all in the directive mode, but the assessment is to be in part collaborative, based on negotiation between trainers and trainees, and in part delegated to trainees to work out their own form of self and peer assessment. So on level 2 all the basic educational decision-making is done in the directive mode with the exception of assessment. This is shown in Figure 1.4. Remember this figure only shows decision-modes used at level 2, the level of planning.

The main method is the use of a business simulation with role play, which runs throughout the five days. The trainees themselves manage a business whose nature and logistics are pre-defined by staff.

On level 1, not shown in Figure 1.4, the learning activity involves a great degree of self-directed initiative and problem-solving among trainees, together with significant collaborative prompting from the trainers, and all within the parameters of the given business simulation. So the methods, designed by direction at level 2, involve a lot of delegation and negotiation in their use on level 1.

	Objectives	Programme	Methods	Resources	Assessment
Direction: Facilitator alone	X	X	X	X	
Negotiation: Facilitator/Learners					X
Delegation: Learners alone					X

Figure 1.4 *Level 2 planning on a UK company course*

The trainers are functioning with some awareness on level 2, but by no means with full awareness, since they simply have not considered the full array of options open to them at level 2. They choose to be mostly directive in planning the learning. This is probably appropriate, but it is by default not by conscious decision.

Second, let's look at a day-release professional development course, for experienced professional helpers, run over several weeks at a UK postgraduate centre. Participants first determine their own personal learning objectives, and these are shared with other participants. In the light of this, facilitator and participants negotiate a final set of objectives, a provisional course programme, learning methods and resources to be used.

The design of assessment procedures is entirely delegated and is to be executed by self and peer assessment among the participants. So here at level 2, objectives, the programme, methods and resources are dealt with by negotiation, assessment by delegation. This is shown in Figure 1.5, which as before only depicts level 2, the level of planning.

	Objectives	Programme	Methods	Resources	Assessment
Direction: Facilitator alone					
Negotiation: Facilitator/Learners	X	X	X	X	
Delegation: Learners alone					X

Figure 1.5 *Level 2 planning at a UK postgraduate centre*

At level 1, the actual training activities involved a lot of structured interpersonal skills exercises. The design of these was done on the spot and combined direction and negotiation: the facilitator designed some basic parts and negotiated other parts with the participants. The exercises were managed by delegation, that is, in autonomous practice groups.

These two examples only scratch the surface of the inexaustible store of models made possible by the modern learning revolution. Access to this store depends above all, in my view, on facilitators realizing that their political authority has now shifted to the subtle business of working awarely and flexibly with different decision-modes at different levels. This enables them very precisely to define the degree to which they can empower their students, and the rate at which they empower them.

The reconciliation of autonomy and holism

I referred earlier to the tension between autonomy and holism especially where students have come from a non-autonomous and non-holistic educational background. If they plan their own learning early in the course they will do so using their old non-holistic learning methods. If, however, students are going to be initiated into holistic methods, then the facilitators will have to plan a lot of the learning.

On a long course of two or more years, the resolution of this tension can be handled in a straightforward conservative way. The first year is planned at level 2 entirely by staff (with the exception of assessment) so that it includes both an extensive use of holistic methods at level 1, and a progressive consciousness-raising among students about how the methods work and how to use them - in effect a gradual delegation of the skill required. At level 1 in the classroom there is, of course, a great deal of student self-direction in managing the prescribed activities within the given format. Any assessment in the first year would be negotiated at level 2 as some form of collaborative assessment involving students and staff.

Comprehensive negotiation at level 2 is introduced in the second year with the use of learning contracts, which cover everything - objectives, programme, methods, resources and assessment. The supposition is that students will now be able to integrate the holistic methods they have acquired in the first year into the learning programmes they devise for these contracts. And since these are *contracts*, staff can prompt students and suggest elements of holism that may have been overlooked, although the primary responsibility is with the student for the first attempt at trying to marry learning objectives and methods into a coherent programme.

Such an overall design for a course would need to be fully explained in the prospectus and at selection interviews, so that students would know what to expect and could choose whether or not to commit themselves to this set of educational values.

A prospectus integrating authority, autonomy and holism

In this section I give an outline of a hypothetical course prospectus which seeks to marry the facilitator's authority with student autonomy and holistic, multi-stranded learning. I present it as the text to be handed to prospective students. I give it here in a much abbreviated form so that the main outline is clear. The actual text would have a lot more detail and an appended programme.

1. Introduction. This is a prospectus for a two-year part-time course on facilitation skills. Each year is made up of three terms. Each term includes ten weekly one-day sessions and three week-end workshops. Each year also includes two five-day workshops. The course offers an educational model that integrates facilitator hierarchy or direction with student autonomy and a holistic, multi-stranded curriculum.

2. The contract. This prospectus constitutes a contract to which all those who enrol on the course will be invited to give their written assent. Please consider it fully and see whether it represents the kind of education which you feel you believe in and can become committed to. At your interview be sure to ask about any aspect of it which is not clear to you. The contract itself is non-negotiable with course members: it provides the framework within which negotiation between facilitator and course members, and the autonomy of the members, can occur.

3. The holistic, multi-stranded curriculum. The course offers a programme of holistic education in which six different strands of learning interweave and run concurrently. These strands are: personal, interpersonal and transpersonal development; theoretical understanding; writing skills; facilitation skills; social change development; political skills internal to the course. The course focusses mainly on the personal, interpersonal and transpersonal development strand in the first two terms, but all the other five strands will be launched alongside it, in particular facilitation skills through co-counselling. The facilitation skills strand is developed more fully from the start of the third term of the first year. The contract requires that all six strands are fully sustained through the second year.

4. Facilitator hierarchy. The facilitators' direction is evident in all the following items: planning the topics and choosing the visiting facilitators for all the nine week-end workshops of the first year; planning (early on by direction, later on by negotiation) and facilitating two-thirds of the content of the weekly meetings throughout the first year, interweaving the six strands; prescribing the amount of written work for both the first and the second years; prescribing a time allocation for facilitation skills in the second year; prescribing that there be a social change project in the second year; and that there be self and peer assessment at the end of each year and self and peer accreditation at the end of the second year. The facilitators will facilitate peer decision-making in the first year, but will progressively delegate this role to course members as the year proceeds. The first year includes training in peer decision-making, self and peer assessment, self and peer accreditation. Throughout the two years the facilitators are the guardians and upholders of this contract.

5. Course member autonomy. Course members negotiate with the facilitators when the latter are using negotiated planning during the weekly meetings in the first year. The members acquire peer decision-making skills in training sessions in the first term; they apply these skills both in the group and as rotating group facilitator in autonomous planning of (i) the one-third of the first-year weekly meetings not planned by the facilitator; (ii) both five-day workshops in the first year; (iii) the *whole* of the second year, including the time allocation for facilitation skills, requirements for written work, and final self and peer assessment and self and peer accreditation. In all this planning, members are subject to the course contract of sustaining the six strands throughout the two years. Course members negotiate with each facilitator about how he or she will fulfil the role of guardian and upholder of the course contract during the second year.

The abbreviated prospectus above involves a dramatic shift from a high facilitator profile in the first year to peer group autonomy in the second year. Planning in the second year goes beyond the use of a learning contract between course members and the facilitator into a much more radical form of self-direction by the course membership. The only contract with the facilitator in the second year is about how he or she will function as guardian and upholder of the contract. So course members have a strong say in how the actual role of the facilitator will be manifested in the second year. Figure 1.6 shows the level 2 planning, with primary planning in bold and secondary in ordinary type.

The main objectives of the course for both years are covered by the six strands and these are part of the course prospectus and so are shown as decided directively. But members' personal versions of these will be decided by delegation, more superfically in the first year and more deeply in the second.

The Year 2 entry in the direction-programme box represents the facilitators' time-allocation for facilitation skills and the social change project requirement in the second year. The Year 2 entry in the negotiation-resources box is the all-important negotiation about how the facilitators are to be used as resources in the second year.

	Objectives	Programme	Methods	Resources	Assessment
Direction: Facilitator alone	Year 1 Year 2	Year 1 Year 2	Year 1	Year 1	
Negotiation: Facilitator/Learners		Year 1	Year 1	Year 1 Year 2	
Delegation: Learners alone	Year 1 Year 2	Year 1 Year 2	Year 1 Year 2	Year 1 Year 2	Year 1 Year 2

Figure 1.6 *Level 2 planning in the integrated prospectus*

Such a design is, of course, controversial. Some people will say that a course on facilitation skills needs much more active supervision by the facilitators throughout the whole two years. Others will hold that the design will enable members to make an autonomous choice of such supervision in the second year, and that this will make it more effective. What is clear is that once mastery of decision-modes is fully available to course designers, we are launched into a new educational era of unexplored forms of empowerment.

Charismatic authority as initiation

The third aspect of authority, charismatic authority, I defined at the outset as the facilitators' influence on learners and the learning process by virtue of their presence, style and manner, that is, through their personal delivery of tutelary and political authority. Charismatic facilitators empower people directly by the presence of their own inner empowerment.

This means eliciting the emergence of the autonomy and wholeness of learners through a behavioural manner, a timing and tone of voice, as well as choice of language and ideas, that proceed from the autonomy and wholeness of the facilitator. It is this expressive presence that generates self-confidence and self-esteem in learners, and enhances their motivation toward independence and integration of being. I address this theme more fully in the next chapter.

2. Charismatic training

Charisma, personal power and personal presence

Charismatic training is about training facilitators to make conscious use of their own personal power. According to the *Shorter Oxford English Dictionary*, the word 'charism' is from the Latin *charisma* and means 'a favour specially vouchsafed by God; a grace, a talent'. In New Testament Greek it means the gift of grace. It was introduced into sociology by Max Weber to refer to an 'extraordinary quality' in persons which gives them a unique and magical impact on others. He distinguished between individual charisma which arises from personal qualities, and the charisma of office which comes from a sacred role.

Weber used the concept in his theory of authority, which included three possible types of legitimacy in a society: traditional, charismatic and legal-rational. If a society becomes too restricted by tradition, change is usually only possible when past customs are challenged by a charismatic leader whose legitimacy derives from his or her personal qualities. Charisma thus has revolutionary power. But when the leader has achieved change it has to be secured by setting up legal-rational legitimacy through an administrative system: secondary persons are endowed with the authority of the leader through the symbols of their office, and so we have the 'routinization of charisma' (Gerth and Mills, 1984).

What I mean by charisma is personal power. I do not mean by such power the ability to control and dominate others, to be a source of oppression. I mean the very opposite: the ability to be empowered by one's own inner resources, the wellspring within, and the ability thereby to elicit empowerment in others.

A very closely related concept is that of personal presence. Persons have presence when there is something about their posture and demeanour, their way of occupying their bodies and their space in a room that draws the attention of those around. Personal power is personal presence in action, set into motion through dynamic interaction with others. But first I will discuss more fully the notion of presence.

It is to do with awareness manifest through physical bearing: the person is in conscious command of how he or she is appearing in space and time. This awareness with command is not distracted by any internal emotional agitation, or by what is going on in the external environment. Being present, then, is about conscious use of the self in and through the various bodily modes that can relate one to other people. I will call these psychophysical modes, since the mind is always involved with them, either in conscious use, or in a half-conscious forgetful state.

A pioneer of conscious use of the self through postural rearrangement was F. M. Alexander, an Australian actor who discovered he could improve the functioning of his larynx by controlling involuntary movements of his head and neck. He developed this into the Alexander Technique (Alexander, 1969; Barlow, 1973; Brennan, 1991; Thame, 1978). His celebrated injunction 'head forward and up' was part of a whole system of unlearning bad postural and motor habits before learning new ones.

While there is some overlap between the Alexander Technique and what I have to say in this chapter about presence and personal power, my approach is more radical, based on a clear distinction between experiential space and physical space.

My account of presence makes it behaviourally accessible to anyone. The notion of charisma, or personal presence in action, is demystified and revealed as the birthright of every person who takes the trouble to practise it. In the next section I give a summary account of the psychophysical modes of relating to others, before moving on to deepen the account of presence.

The psychophysical modes of relating to others

Figure 2.1 illustrates the primary psychophysical modes of interpersonal encounter. To call these modes of relating to others 'psychophysical' is to say that they are never merely physical, but always informed by greater or lesser intentionality and awareness. They are forms of mental and personal as well as physical expression.

1. Posture. Posture or bearing is about how people hold their trunk, limbs, head and neck as a whole when standing, sitting or reclining. When taken into motion, posture becomes carriage or gait.

2. Gesture. I have in mind here primarily the use of the hands and arms; but this can extend to include movements of the trunk, head and neck, and occasionally a foot. Hand and arm gestures can be purely expressive: they are not intended to convey meaning, but simply to provide an aesthetic accompaniment to the spoken word. Or they can be indicative, and have a purpose: to beckon, halt, point, outline, and so on. Some indicative gestures may also be expressive.

3. Facial expression. The face can be in repose, as when looking at the world, or listening attentively to another person; or it can be animated as when talking and active in conversational exchange, or in emotional arousal. Its expression depends on how the muscles of the jaw, mouth, nose, eyes and brow interact.

4. Relative position. There are three dimensions of the position of one person relative to another. The first is distance: they can be near or far, from being close

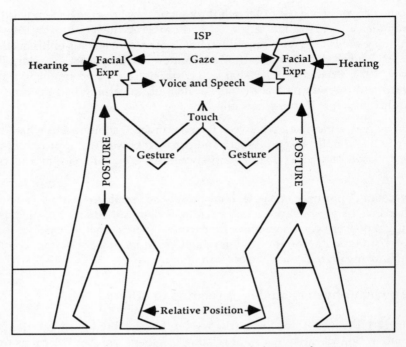

Figure 2.1 *The psychophysical modes of relating to others*

up to being at the other end of the room. The second is height: they can be above or below or at the same level; for example, one standing when the other is sitting, or both sitting. The third is orientation: they can be face to face; beside on the right or on the left, and either facing the same way or opposite ways; face to back, or back to back. These three dimensions can combine in innumerable ways.

5. Voice. By voice I mean the paralinguistic aspects of speech, that is, how a person speaks as distinct from what they say. This includes physical tone or timbre, volume, pitch, rate of speech, rhythm of speech, use of inflection and emphasis, use of silence and pauses, emotional tone. The variations and combinations of these provide a powerful nonverbal vocal language, which can be used to influence strongly what is being said.

6. Speech. This covers what a person says, the meaning of the words used. It also refers to how language is used: the choice of words and grammatical structures.

7. Hearing. Hearing has three aspects: listening to how the other speaks, to the various dimensions of voice; listening to what they are saying, to the content of their speech; and listening to the linguistic structure of their speech, that is, the choice of words and of grammatical structures.

8. Gazing. I refer here to the use of the eyes, which is twofold. I can look at your behaviour, that is, at your posture, gestures, facial expression, relative position. Or I can look into your eyes, which, if they are looking into mine, will involve mutual gazing. Mutual gazing may be less or more mutual. One person may be dominant in the gaze, the other transfixed into temporary passivity and submission; or both persons may be equally engaged in projecting and receiving. In the latter case, mutual gazing is one form of immediate encounter with another human being: it enables true meeting to occur, since both persons are in simultaneous, reciprocal contact. I gaze at and receive your gaze, which is gazing at and receiving mine: four acts are happening all at once.

9. Touch. I may touch you in the dominant mode, when you are entirely passive and receptive, as when I lay my hand on your shoulder. Or we may touch each other with full reciprocity as when we shake hands. This last is the other form of immediate encounter between human beings: I give my touch and receive your touch while you do the same. Four processes occur simultaneously.

10. Smell. There are gender differences here. Assuming basic hygiene, women are more aware than men of intrinsic biological smell. In ordinary social intercourse, this is not a channel of communication that is highly significant at the conscious level. Nevertheless, there may be strong subliminal influences which have an effect on behaviour. Also the use by both sexes of deodorants, by men of after-shave lotions, and by women of perfumes, may influence mutual perceptions and appraisals.

11. Taste. As a mode of relating to others, taste is normally restricted to intimate, erotic encounters.

12. Intrasensory perception. By intrasensory perception, ISP for short, I mean a non-sensory apprehension of the other's mental and emotional state, which is interwoven with sensory apprehesion but cannot be reduced to it. Thus the gaze is mediated by the eyes, but is not the eyes; personal touch is mediated by tactile sensation but is not identical with it; feeling the experiential space and energy field of the other is not the same as observing their posture and is not an inference from it, but a non-sensory apprehension interwoven with it - hence the term intrasensory. ISP is symbolized in Figure 2.1 by the inclusive circle over the two people.

The basic distinction in this list is between speech - the use of language to convey meaning - and all the other nonverbal modes including voice. Thomas Reid, the Scottish philosopher of common sense, likewise distinguished between the artificial language of words and the natural language of 'modulations of voice, gestures and features'. These latter signs, he held, are naturally expressive of our thoughts and it is by them we give force and energy to our use of words. Words 'signify but do not express, they speak to the understanding, but the passions, affections and the will hear them not; these continue dormant and inactive until we speak to them in the language of nature to which they are all attention and obedience'.

Reid also thought that the 'vocabulary' of natural language, that is, what nonverbal signs mean, is everywhere the same and intelligible without having to be learnt. The knowledge of it is latent in the mind and a precondition of being able to develop verbal language (Reid, 1764).

The experiential body and the physical body

The most basic of the psychophysical modes of relating to others, since it is the ground of all the others, is posture - how you hold and carry yourself and occupy your space. This spatial disposition, or physical attitude, is informed by a mental attitude which is conveyed to attentive observers. This bodily manifested state of mind reveals a great deal of information about persons: how they feel about themselves and the world around them. And it makes a statement to other people about all that.

When you use total body posture awarely, you do so by feeling where every part of your body is in relation to every other part, and where the whole is in space and on the ground. This feeling is organized as your inner body-image, which must be distinguished from your outer body-image. The latter is derived from what you look like from outside: from what you can see of yourself, from mirror images and from feedback from others about your appearance.

The inner body-image is the one you live in: you inhabit it when you stand and sit and move and lie down. It is your *felt sense* of how you are distributed in space and grounded on the earth. It is comprised of integrated kinaesthetic and proprioceptive imagery. I shall call it the experiential body: the body known in terms of inner feeling and experience. The outer body-image, known by your looking and by the perception of others, I shall call the physical body. Figure 2.2 illustrates the difference between the two.

The experiential body, as well as providing immediate inner experience of your physical body and its disposition in space, is also a form of consciousness. I am talking in non-Cartesian terms here: consciousness as spatial extension. The mind pervades and is manifested in the space of the experiential body. When you are fully aware throughout the experiential body, upholding physical bearing with that consciousness, then you manifest personal presence.

It is clear that the experiential body is spatially extended awareness: if it were not so we could have no inner knowledge of how the physical body is disposed in space. It is also clear that the experiential body interpenetrates and is distinct from the physical body. The interpenetration guarantees awareness and control of physical location. The distinction between the two is evident in the fact that while you can prod and slap my physical leg and measure it, you cannot do the same to my extended felt sense of where that leg is. You can stick a pin in my body, but not in my experience of my body.

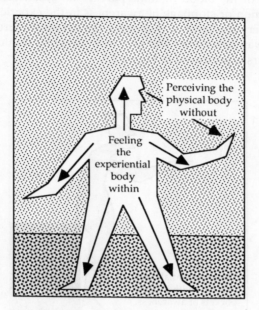

Perceiving the physical body without

Feeling the experiential body within

Figure 2.2 *The experiential body and the physical body*

Deriving from the distinction between the experiential body and the physical body is the distinction between experiential space and physical space. Experiential space is known by indwelling it, by feeling it as a whole and from within, simultaneously. Such indwelling is in principle illimitable, of unknown potential range. Physical space is known perceptually, serially in terms of piecemeal views, perspectives and orientations, through vision, hearing, touch and by moving from one part of it to another. Experiential space complements physical space, interpenetrating it and enhancing it with a four-dimensional all-at-once grasp of its three dimensions.

The experiential body in stasis

Many facilitators are crouching unawarely, forgetful and half-asleep, in their experiential bodies and their physical posture shows the unmistakable signs of this: the head and jaw too far forward, stature reduced, the anterior thorax too concave and withdrawn, the pelvis and thighs posturally negated. Such a person is about to talk too much, exhibits anxious overcontrol and is missing a lot of what is going on in the group energy field around.

In this condition, the experiential body is in stasis. In conventional pathology, stasis is a stagnation or stoppage of the circulation of any of the fluids of the body, especially of the blood in some part of the blood-vessels. By analogy, there is a stagnation or stoppage of awareness in the experiential body. Some parts of it have very low level of awareness: the felt sense there is almost asleep. In other parts, awareness comes and goes in an irregular fashion here and there. This state of affairs is portrayed in Figure 2.3.

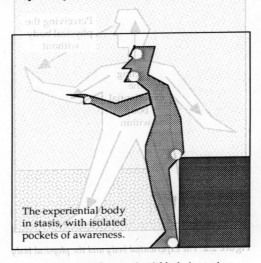

The experiential body
in stasis, with isolated
pockets of awareness.

Figure 2.3 *The experiential body in stasis*

When you are crouching in this way in your experiential body, your awareness in it is reduced and disjointed, occurring in disconnected pockets. So if you are dimly slumped in a chair with ankles crossed, and head jutting forward, you have a low level oscillating awareness of lumps of yourself here and other parts there. To take this sort of stasis into the facilitator role is to have little or no presence and to appear mainly as a talking head.

The experiential body in presence

Charisma or presence occurs to a remarkable degree simply when people arouse themselves from inner slumber and occupy the total experiential body with full consciousness. What is distinctive about this awareness is that it is holistic. It occurs all at once. It is a concurrent knowing of where all the parts are and of their integrated volume, their gesture in space. It is not an external, perceived, perspectival knowing of form, but an internal, felt, simultaneous grasp of a total three-dimensional pattern. It is living geometric awareness of one's place in space.

Head, neck and spine are arranged in such a way that there is a subtle unifying sense of lift and levity running through the whole, an expansive lengthening and widening of the back; pelvis, thighs and legs are grounded in awareness of the floor below. This harmonious integration of levity and gravity is managed from the *hara*, the vital centre in the abdomen just below the level of the navel. F. M. Alexander got on to the idea of what he called the primary control - 'the head, neck, back relationship' - for co-ordinated posture (Brennan, 1991: 21). Practice in the martial art of Aikido brings out the role of the *hara* as the organizing centre for this relationship and all others in the experiential body so that there is a felt sense of it as a liberated integrated gesture in space, encompassing a free flow of subtle energy.

When a person does this very simple act of using the will to be synchronously aware within the whole experiential body, then he or she has moved from an ordinary, slouched and impotent state, to an altered, commanding and potent state of being. It is as if the experiential body, thus aroused as a fully extended form of consciousness, radiates its subtle energy, permeating those around and subliminally eliciting their attention. It also means, of course, that the person is ready to feel the spatial, energetic and social field beyond the confines of his or her physical body. The facilitator in this state is poised at the verge of pervasive interpersonal empathy. It is also as if in this state a person refracts something of his or her archetypal nature, *ipsissimus* or *ipsissima*.

A facilitator who is experientially aware throughout his or her posture, who feels its totality, the complete gesture it makes in space, exhibits unmistakable presence. This is the foundation of charisma. And, as if the will is the rotating knob on a rheostat, you can increase or decrease the energy of awareness, the conscious charge, within the felt experiential body, and so enhance or reduce the charismatic impact.

From here on in several of the sections of this chapter, I give a sample of some of the exercises I use in charismatic training sessions for people to enhance different aspects of their personal presence and power.

Exercise 1. Stand up and arrange your experiential body so that you can be present throughout it all at once. Find your way into the exhilarating feeling of simultaneous extension in all directions. Your posture will assume a stance like those found in the *mudras* (sacred postures) of Tantric practice, or in the martial arts such as Tai Chi and Aikido: knees somewhat bent, legs well grounded, arms out from the side, elbows bent; spine, neck and head aligned with a subtle feeling of levity, the back elongated and widened. Now move slowly, maintaining this same experiential presence throughout your moving form, co-ordinating the integrated, extended awareness from the *hara*, the centre of gravity - and levity - within the lower abdomen. Form into pairs and share your findings with each other. End with experience-sharing in the whole group.

Exercise 2. Work together in pairs and stand opposite each other. In silence, without any dialogue, one person practise shutting down and opening up full awareness in the experiential body, moving their mental attitude to and fro several times from being slouched half-asleep in it to being fully present throughout it. When moving into presence in this exercise stay within the limits of 'normal' posture. Give a report on the felt difference between these two states of being, then hear feedback from your partner. Reverse roles. End with experience-sharing in the whole group.

From personal presence to personal power

In the opening section to this chapter, I defined personal power in two overlapping ways: first, as the ability to be empowered by one's own inner resources, the wellspring within, and the ability thereby to elicit empowerment in others; and second, as personal presence in action, set into motion through dynamic relation with others. You can manifest total presence when in the company of others, yet not engage in any kind of explicit social intercourse. When you start to interact with others, you can either take your presence into personal power, or disappear into conventional social behaviour.

Personal power is rather like the original light of the soul taking charge of its earthly location and its human relationships. Our whole culture runs a strong tacit taboo which conditions people to bury such a propensity and keep it repressed, and to feel diffident and embarrassed when invited to manifest it. This awkwardness, hidden behind conventional social behaviour, is very strong. So the move from being silently present to actively manifesting personal power is problematic.

In terms of the psychophysical modes of relating, what is called for is the integration of posture, gesture, facial expression including the gaze, with relative position, hearing, voice and, of course, speech. Human beings are multi-modal beings and have a great facility for integrating many different psychological and interactive modes in one effortless performance, even if much of the time they do this forgetfully and half-asleep from the point of view of personal power. So it is not the integrated mastery that is difficult, but the release from embarrassment and conventional comatose habit.

The up-hierarchy of empowerment

What is needed is a radical strategy for releasing the inner wellspring so that people are inwardly empowered, and feel both the exhilaration of this and the rapport with others that it engenders. This strategy is provided by the up-hierarchy of empowerment, which is the key to charismatic training and can readily be turned into dynamic experience.

An up-hierarchy works from below upwards, like a tree with roots, a trunk, branches and fruit. It is not a matter of the higher controlling and ruling the lower, as in a down-hierarchy, but of the higher branching and flowering out of, and bearing the fruit of, the lower. The basic features of an up-hierarchy are these: what is higher is tacit and latent in what is lower; the lowest level is the formative potential of higher levels; the higher levels emerge out of the lower; there are many different possible forms of emergence; the higher levels are a reduced precipitate of the lower; each level has a relative autonomy within the total system; what is lower grounds, supports and nourishes what is higher.

It is my belief that the developed human psyche functions as an up-hierarchy, in which the grounding level is that of feeling, construed as the capacity for resonance with being and participative attunement to other beings. Out of this affective mode emerges the imaginal mode, including the imagery of imagination, memory and perception. From the imaginal proceeds the conceptual mode, the domain of thought and language; and this is the basis for the development of the practical mode, the level of intention and action. This view has been thoroughly worked out in another book (Heron, 1992) and I must refer the reader to it for the details.

When this up-hierarchy model is applied to the empowerment of the psychophysical modes of relating to others, then we have the following levels. In terms of a spatial metaphor, level 1 is *below* level 2 and so on, and power and influence proceeds from below upwards.

Level 1. The grounding level is that of feeling the fullness of your presence, as already described: you are experientially extended, all at the same time, throughout your posture, feeling its totality, the complete gesture it makes in space. This feeling of presence in your posture will integrate with it your gestures, facial expression including the use of the gaze, your position relative to the other, and your listening, and will extend to pervade empathically the total presence of the group and of members within it. This feeling is the well-spring of the up-hierarchy, the source out of which all the other stages emerge.

Level 2. Allow this integrated feeling of personal and interactive presence to shape when and to whom you speak, the whole pattern of the timing and tone of your voice and of the phonetic sound you make. Voice, remember, is to do with how you speak, as distinct from what you say. By the timing of your voice, I mean a combination of the following: the speed at which you speak, the rhythm of your speech, the use of inflection and emphasis, and the use of pauses and silences. By the tone of your voice, I mean mainly the emotional tone, but include also physical tone or timbre, volume and pitch. And by the pattern of sounds you make, I mean literally the shape of the noises, the phonemes, that come out of your mouth. The idea at this stage is to let the total pattern of timing, tone of voice and phonetics well up out of feeling fully present as described in level 1.

Level 3. Now let the timing and tone of voice and pattern of sound of level 2 shape the choice of words and grammatical structures, the linguistic pattern you use. And let this in turn influence what you say, the ideas and information, judgments and opinions you put forward.

Level 4. Finally, allow your intentions and purposes in relating to the other to be shaped and moulded by the cumulative impact of all the prior levels of the up-hierarchy.

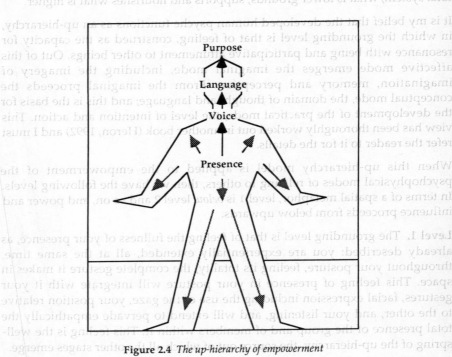

Figure 2.4 *The up-hierarchy of empowerment*

Figure 2.4 shows the up-hierarchy of empowerment. In this figure, 'presence' refers to everything in level 1, 'voice' to the timing, tone and sound of voice in level 2, 'language' to both the choice and meaning of words in level 3, and 'purpose' to the intentions involved in relating to the other at level 4.

This is, of course, a complete reversal of the conventional approach to relating to another person. The normal thing is to have some purpose in mind in approaching the other, to let this shape the content of what you are going to say, which in turn will select the words and linguistic structures, which will influence the tone, timing and sounds of voice; then posture, gesture, facial expression and relative position will adapt accordingly. This is the normal down-hierarchy influence in human interaction.

I am not suggesting that this down-hierarchy is simply to be abandoned. It is in any case too habitual, too ingrained in social intercourse for that. What I propose is that the trainee facilitator disattend from it, and empower him or herself with conscious use of the up-hierarchy, and learn how empowering it is for the other to be the recipient of that conscious use. In a later section I discuss the integration of the two hierarchies.

For purposes of clarity in the exposition, I have described the four levels of the up-hierarchy as if they follow one after the other in a temporal sequence: first you do this and then the next and so on. But this is obviously not what actually happens. While level 1, that of postural presence, clearly comes first in time, the other levels come all at once. What the up-hierarchy is pointing to is an order of influence, what is simultaneously grounded in what. It indicates whence and how the empowerment proceeds.

Integrated postural presence

Level 1 of the up-hierarchy is as I have said the grounding level. I characterized it as being 'experientially extended, all at the same time, throughout your posture, feeling its totality, the complete gesture it makes in space', and described it further in the earlier section on 'The experiential body in presence'. Let me say here what this does not mean in postural terms.

Many facilitators who have not done any charismatic training tend toward the following postural distortion: the neck is taut, the head and jaw are pushed too far forward and down, the masseter muscle of the jaw is sometimes too tense; the back is reduced in length; the chest is concave and the heart area negated and disowned; the lower abdomen and the whole of the pelvic area and upper thighs are disregarded, by a buried position in a chair, with legs inertly crossed. The same distortions continue when the person stands - neck taut, head and jaw forward and down, the stature reduced, chest caved in, and the lower body energetically alienated. It is virtually impossible to get awareness and presence going with this posture: the experiential body of the person concerned is in chronic stasis.

Some trainees need physically rearranging to discover the power latent in their presence. So I gently move the chest forward inviting the person to extend the thoracic spine a little, spread the chest and move the heart forwards and *offer it to the group*. This makes the head and jaw less cantilevered, more appropriately forward and up, aligns, lifts and liberates the spine and neck, widens the back, and interrupts the compulsion anxiously to talk too much in clock time. Then I invite them to sit upright grounded on the chair with legs uncrossed, feet earthed and thighs apart, to own the whole of the lower half of the body, letting its energy enrich their presence, and to organize the total gesture in space from the lower abdomen. It is very noticeable how simply getting into this postural re-alignment will by itself dramatically alter how a person uses their voice and what they say in their speech.

The heart is full of psychophysical energy and so is the pelvis. These energies need to be the ground for the energies of the throat and the head in integrated postural presence. People need quite a lot of encouragement to open up and evoke these energies and get them going in manifest presence and personal power.

Postural presence, being dynamic and holistic, will integrate with it your gestures and facial expression including the use of the gaze, since these things are all integral parts of the experiential body. It will also integrate your position relative to the other, and your listening, and I deal with these in the next section.

Exercise 1. People work in pairs. Each partner takes a turn doing all the following, first seated and then standing: place your left hand on your lower abdomen and say 'I am present in my belly' and occupy awarely the whole of the lower experiential body; then on your chest and say 'I am present in my heart', while entering thoracic space and integrating it with the lower body; then on your larynx and say 'I am present in my voice', while entering the throat, integrating it with the thorax and the lower body; then on your forehead and say 'I am present in my head' re-aligning the head, neck and spine with the larynx, the chest and the lower body; finally, while feeling the total integrated posture from within, affirm the four statements one after the other, ending with the statement 'I am present'. Follow with report from self on the experience and feedback from partner. End with experience-sharing in the whole group.

Exercise 2. People work seated in pairs. Each partner takes a turn at role playing any short piece of facilitator talk, speaking it first of all crouched in a typical state of postural stasis, and then again with integrated postural presence, ending with a report from self on the experience followed by feedback from partner. End with experience-sharing in the whole group.

Pervasive interpersonal empathy

When the experiential body is fully awake as an extended form of consciousness, the person is thereby attuned to the whole of the immediate spatial and social environment. To be entirely here now is also to be entirely there now. Presence at the centre yields attunement at the periphery. To feel from within the total gesture your body is making in space means also that your awareness is beyond that gesture: it interpenetrates holistically the spatial field around you. You are aware of your position in relation to others, and you are aware of others - not simply perceptually but by a subtle interpenetration of their own experiential space. You are in a state of pervasive interpersonal empathy. You are listening to others.

In the literal sense of 'listening' you are hearing what people are saying and how they are saying it: you are attending to speech and voice in others. In an extended and metaphorical sense, you are 'hearing' how they are being in their own experiential space: you are resonating with them, attuning to them, feeling their way of manifesting themselves in the moment. We call this rapport.

Egan in his fourth edition of *The Skilled Helper* writes of 'social-emotional presence' by which he means giving full attention to the client, combined with verbal and nonverbal behaviour which indicates 'a clear-cut willingness to work with the client'. This is backed up by an awareness of one's body as a source of communication, and by what he calls 'microskills' which include facing the client squarely, adopting an open posture, leaning forwards or backwards to enhance responsiveness to the client, maintaining good eye contact, and being relatively relaxed in these behaviours. He thinks this microskills level is 'the most superficial level of attending' (Egan, 1990: 108-111). This last is surely a mistaken view, mainly because Egan has not penetrated to the heart of presence - which is how a person simultaneously feels his or her total gesture in space. It is this whole way of being here now, reaching out to embrace the client, that is the foundation of rapport.

What underlies rapport is the fact that experiential space, the holistic space of the experiential body which we feel all at once, extends to interpenetrate surrounding space in order to be able to know the total gesture being made in that space. To know from within the total shape your body is making in space, means that you also know the spatial field around it from within. This capacity to feel the 'within' of space around us, and so to feel interpenetration and resonance with the experiential space of other beings, is, I believe, a fundamental capacity of human personhood (Heron, 1992). We are inherently empathic, resonating, attuning, spatially interpenetrating beings: we can know each other through this subtle compenetration - shared participation in experiential space - as well as through perceptual encounter in physical space. What our culture does is to fixate our attention on the latter and suppress our capacity for the former. Figure 2.5 illustrates a shared experiential spatial field.

A deeper view is that there is one universal experiential multispace, the presence of a cosmic consciousness interpenetrating, upholding and including physical space; that each person is a local and limited experiential space within it; and that there is in reality no gap, no barrier between the immediate experiential space of individual personal presences, nor between them and the experiential multispace of cosmic presence.

In face-to-face shared rapport there is compenetration of presence, a mutual indwelling by each of his or her own and the other's experiential space. There is participation in one common experiential field with two distinct foci. Sometimes the rapport may be more consciously one-way, as with facilitators doing one-to-one counselling or working intensively with one person in front of a group. In this case their felt participation in the experiential space of the other is the ground for their practice of active empathy. It heightens their ability to attend not just to the meaning of what is being said, but also to how it is being said - the tone of voice, choice of language, emotional emphases and inflections, redundancies and slips of the tongue. And it enables them to notice all the bodily cues - the rate and depth of breathing, use of eye contact, facial expression, rigidities or labilities of gesture and posture - which reveal how the person is being, both consciously and unconcsciously.

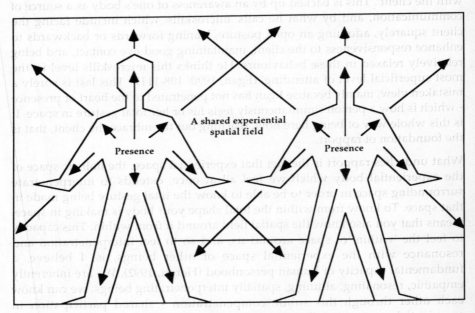

Figure 2.5 *A shared experiential spatial field*

Huxley (1963) thought that empathy was strictly a metaphysical impossibility because, he said, we are all private island universes, yet he also held it was necessary and possible by inference or feeling into others. This conflicted and confused view is quoted by Egan (1990: 123) and seems to be echoed by Margulies (1984: 1030) who writes of empathy as a 'negation of self' and thinks it 'involves a kind of self-aggression'. Theodor Lipps thought our belief in the existence of other minds is based on an empathic projection of self into the physical manifestations of others. And generally empathy is defined as a projection of self into the feelings of others. The word itself was coined by

Vernon Lee in 1904 and used by Titchener as a translation of the German *Einfühlung*, 'feeling into'.

I think empathy is much better defined as an immediate felt apprehension of the psychophysical states of others. It is a participative kind of direct knowing. It involves neither inference, nor a projection of self into the feelings of others if this is meant to imply that we assume the form of those feelings and thus know them only indirectly. Max Scheler's account of our knowledge of other minds as direct perception, in which we see a complex whole consisting of the physical expression and what it expresses, comes nearer the truth of the matter. He argues cogently against inference and self projection theories of how we know that other minds exist (Scheler, 1954).

I suspect that the reduction of empathy to a kind of self-bound projection is all to do with the experiential body being in stasis, with a lack of cultivation of the total feeling of one's gesture in the surround of experiential space. For it is this which yields felt participation in the experiential space of other people.

Exercise 1. This exercise is a piece of homework. At a later time park your car in a limited space between two other parked cars. Practise doing this by becoming aware of the experiential form of the car, of the space it is to enter, and of the relative positions of the two. So you have a felt sense of the whole configuration of car and parking space known all at once from within. Indwell this configuration while manoeuvring the car, supported of course by visual perspectives in physical space. Note the greater ease with which you can park the car when doing so with presence, compared with trying to manoeuvre it exclusively from limited physical perspectives.

Exercise 2. People work in pairs. Partners move slowly and silently around each other: become conscious within the shared experiential space that includes the total postures and relative positions of each of you. Practise sustaining this all-at-once grasp of shared experiential space while facing and looking at the other, while side by side and catching only a glimpse of the other in the corner of the visual field, and while being back to back and unable to see the other. The challenge is not to get sucked back into attending entirely to perceived perspectives in physical space. Experience-sharing in pairs and then in the whole group.

Exercise 3. People work in pairs. Partners approach each other, shake hands and say 'Hello', all the while having a felt sense of the total spatial form of the two person interaction from within your shared experiential space. Often the handshake and the 'Hello' will throw you out of experiential space awareness into restricted physical space awareness. So keep practising until your consciousness is no longer distracted and contracted by the social convention. Experience-sharing in pairs and then in the whole group.

Exercise 4. People work in groups of four and for several minutes have an informal conversation on what has been going on so far in the training programme. At the same time practise indwelling, in experiential space, the whole shared configuration of the group, feeling from within it everyone's total spatial gesture in relation with everyone else's. Ordinary social interaction has built into it hidden norms of contracted spatial awareness, of living in space as exclusively perceptual and physical. So during the conversation you need to remind yourself to resist these tacit norms, and stay in subtle expanded inner space. Experience-sharing in the small groups and then in the whole group.

Exercise 5. People work in pairs. Partners take it in turns to talk for some minutes about your plans for their next main holiday. As listener practise being aware within the whole of your own experiential body and expand this to include awareness of the relative positions of both of you, this spatial configuration being felt as a whole from within it. Then you indwell more particularly the experiential space of the speaker and get a felt sense of how he or she is being and manifesting within that space, noticing how this correlates with all the perceived cues of breathing, posture, gesture, facial expression, voice and speech. After each turn, the listeners share their experience with their partners. End with experience-sharing in the whole group.

Exercise 6. Work in the whole group if it is not too large, or in two sub-groups each in a room of its own. Everyone in turn comes and stands at the front of the group and talks for a minute or two in a role play making opening statements in some group they are about to run. When it is your turn, practise being fully present throughout your experiential body and extend this to include the whole shared experiential space of the room with everybody in it. If your awareness contracts back into exclusive physical perception, just gently expand it again. A short report after each turn, then general discussion at the end.

Dynamic interpersonal geometry

Rapport - compenetration with people in experiential space - means that you the facilitator are fully aware of your position relative to everyone else in the group. It also means you are free to move around within this shared space using its dynamic interpersonal geometry.

The group is seated in a circle; you are aware of its shape, of where you and your chair are in relation to each person. You may remain seated; you may stand in front of your chair or behind it; you may move to the centre of the circle or across it to one or more persons; you may move round the circle on the outside of it and stand at various points beyond its perimeter; you may swap chairs with one person in order to sit beside another; you may work with someone standing, sitting or kneeling in front of them, on their right or their left side, very close or more distant.

All these options and many more open up as forms of enriching the facilitation process. The impulse to use shared experiential space within a group in this way comes from within that space: it moves you with its own dynamic currents. I cannot give rules or guiding principles for doing it. Remember that you are moving primarily in the 'within' of space, the felt sense of the shared experiential space of the group, and only secondarily in the physical space of visual perspectives. If you stay in this 'within' of space, people will feel subliminally what you are about, and will be subtly liberated by it.

Exercise. People work in small groups of six. Everyone takes a turn as facilitator in a role play choosing some important piece of facilitation they normally do. In your turn establish yourself in your personal presence and in pervasive rapport with the group, and indwell this shared experiential space while doing your facilitation. Give yourself permission to move freely within this space throughout the facilitation without worrying at all about whether it is fitting or appropriate to go here or go there; just follow the currents. After your turn give yourself feedback, and hear feedback from the group. End with experience-sharing in the whole group.

Clock time and charismatic time

In the sequential account of the up-hierarchy, I suggested that at level 2 what is born out of the integrated presence of level 1 is the timing of speech which as well as the rate at which you speak includes the rhythm of your speech, the use of inflection and emphasis, and the insertion of pauses and silences. For the facilitator there are two basic sorts of speaking time: clock time and charismatic time.

Clock time is rapid speech time, the one used in most teaching and most conversation. It conveys information, belief, evaluation and opinion in fairly long bursts delivered non-stop. It tends to be verbally dense, cognitively loaded, somewhat urgent and in a subtle way over-tense. Most facilitators use it most of the time, since it is the norm for the culture.

One reason why it is urgent and over-tense is because it is being used to displace anxiety about facilitator performance. Another less obvious but equally important reason is that it is also being used, unconsciously, as a defence against the possibility of moving into a totally different way of speaking - in charismatic time.

Speech in charismatic time is deep rhythm speech. The use of the voice is imaginatively shaped and moulded out of the speaker's living presence. It is born out of his or her conscious grounding, being fully here in the space of the world. It is much slower than clock time use of the voice, contains clear rhythmic inflections and the intentional insertion of pauses and silences. A pause is a momentary cessation of speech in the interests of rhythm and emphasis. A silence is a longer pause pregnant with intention and awareness, entirely free of all urgency or tension.

The tone of voice is warmer, richer, deeper, more mellow. With the slower more rhythmic delivery, the altered tone and the use of well-timed silences, the choice of words becomes more basic, the language becomes richer in imagery, tinged with the poetic. The listener is more deeply engaged with the content: he or she is imaginatively involved in what is being said, has time to understand and assimilate it and get interested. In short, the listener starts to feel empowered.

The rapidity of clock-time speech, and its inability to use intentional silence, serves in general social intercourse to displace a good deal of continuous tension. Facilitators, as I have said, use it for the same purpose and therefore tend to say too much for too long - which is inevitable if the purpose of speaking at an unconscious level is to relieve anxiety. So facilitators in training need both to reduce the overall amount they say in clock time, and to learn to speak, as appropriate, in charismatic time.

For a facilitator to say everything in charismatic time would become unbearably pompous, and tedious for the listeners. But to say everything in clock time, which is the current norm, leaves everyone impoverished and unempowered, as if there is a hidden conspiracy, to which all are subservient, that the depths of human reality shall be ignored. What is needed is a facility for moving between the two kinds of speech, which are symbolized in Figure 2.6.

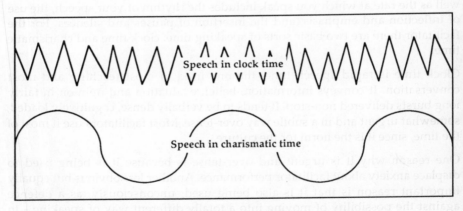

Figure 2.6 *Speech in clock time and in charismatic time*

The use of charismatic time is appropriate for culture-setting statements such as proposing group values and ground-rules; for making contracts about basic objectives and methods; for making important permission-giving statements - for example, to the wounded child within the participants; for implanting suggestions into the group consciousness and process; for handling critical incidents in the group process; and for all those interventions which affirm participants' basic humanity. It is not that you, the facilitator, are continually in charismatic time, but you are modulating the voice into it on occasion, to say things of human depth and significance - during the exposition of some basic ideas, at crucial moments in introducing the deeper point of an exercise, in underlining a vital piece of feedback, in appreciating what has been said or done, and so on.

A key issue in such use is that your voice becomes anxiety-free: it is charged with the power of your presence; it is pregnant with who you really are. The tone, the rhythm, the slower speed reveal that some deeper, confident reality within you is in charge of your manner of delivery: you have empowered your behaviour from a wellspring within, which the up-hierarchy has liberated. It is this nonverbal manner to which above all people respond: it is the real language to which the soul of the listener responds. Once a person feels empowered by this, then he or she is ready to do business positively with the content of what is being said. But if the nonverbal manner of voice and posture is precipitate and anxious, the listener is already predisposed to have difficulty with the content of speech. This is the simple and fundamental point which in my experience many facilitators have not, in practical action, grasped.

The crucial test of competence in the use of charismatic time is the ability to be fully present, without any anxiety, during the intentional silences within your delivery. When people practise charismatic speech, they can shift into appropriate speed, rhythm and tone of voice, but often baulk at the use of significant silence, since residual anxiety is confronted by this.

The thing to do in the silence is to feel your presence, to beam it out through posture, gesture, facial expression, the use of the gaze and relative position, and in and through this very process to be fully attuned to the presence of all your listeners, knowing in this inner deed their fullness of being in the depths of the silence. Empowered within, you are empowering without. In training, I have found it useful to encourage trainees to feel the silence in terms of several of their own heart-beats.

The purpose of a silence, which in fact lasts for no more than two or three seconds, is to underline what has been said, to let its unstated implications unfurl, to let it generate imaginal and emotional resonance, to honour the reality of the listeners - giving them time to take in what you are saying and respond to how you are being and to start to process all this within, and to affirm that the relationship of being together is more basic than speech.

Speaking in clock time also requires attention in training. People need practice in talking in clock time, without going on too long, and ridding it of the cooped-up smell of anxiety and tension. When facilitators are at ease with themselves in their presence, then their clock time speech is more laid back, briefer. If they are not in this way at ease with themselves, they often say too much. Yet it *always* clear to the attentive listener when they have said just the right amount and should stop.

Exercise 1. I invite people to work in pairs; and I have a small gong. Partners take turns over several minutes of describing the place where they live. I have instructed them to start the description in ordinary clock time mode, and that at the first stroke of the gong they are to shift over, continuing the description in charismatic time. At the next stroke of the gong they go back into clock time and so on. The listener just listens, but uses hand gestures to slow the speaker down if charismatic speech degenerates back into clock speech. After each turn, the speaker gives his or her report on the experience, followed by feedback from the listener. End with experience-sharing in the whole group.

Exercise 2. People work in groups of four or five. Each person takes a turn as facilitator in a short role play practising the use of charismatic timing in one of the areas mentioned: culture-setting statements, making contracts, permission-giving statements, implanting suggestions, handling critical incidents, the exposition of some basic ideas, the deeper point of an exercise, underlining a vital piece of feedback, and so on. Each person chooses whichever of these is most pertinent. A paragraph of delivery is sufficient; then feedback to self, feedback from peers, and several re-runs to take account of feedback and deepen the practice. End with experience-sharing in the whole group.

Exercise 3. People work in groups of four or five. Each person takes a turn as facilitator in a short role play practising the use of speaking in clock time to introduce some exercise (a) describing how to do it and (b) giving the rationale for doing it. Each listener puts up a hand when they feel the facilitator has said enough about (a), and likewise about (b). The facilitator stops both (a) and (b) whenever he or she feels it is appropriate to do so. Each turn is followed by feedback to self and feedback from the others. The feedback can consider not only the length of speech, but also any undertow of tension and anxiety. End with experience-sharing in the whole group.

Emotional tone of voice

At level 2 in the up-hierarchy I mentioned tone of voice alongside timing, and said that I mean mainly the emotional tone, but include also physical tone or timbre, volume and pitch. The emotional tone of the voice can convey many different qualities: the tone can be warm or cold, lively or dull, interested or bored, and so on. It is quite distinct from physical tone or timbre: a voice can sound physically like a foghorn or a French horn, yet each of these different timbres can carry a wide range of varied emotional tones.

For some people, the emotional tone of voice gets hijacked by early traumatic history. There gets incorporated in it a chronic inflection of pleading or defiance or whatever other defensive attitude the wounded child adopted in order to survive. This inflection is present whatever the person is saying in whatever circumstance. It is not clear why this defensive displacement occurs in some and not in others. But if a facilitator has it, then it makes sense to retrain the voice and become free of it, otherwise participants in groups will be thrown subliminally into parent-type transference by it. If at the same time because of other aspects of what the facilitator is doing they are cast into child-type transference, then they are going to be in a bit of a muddle.

Physical tone, or timbre, is to do with the structure of the voice-box and of the resonating cavities, and as I say is independent of emotional tone in the sense that the same basic timbre can carry many very different emotional tones. However, there is also an important connection between them. Timbre is a product of the proportion in which the fundamental tone is combined with the harmonics or overtones. There is not much I can do about the basic structures of my voice-box and related parts which produce the fundamental tone. But there is a great deal I can do about two closely related things: how I put the breath through the voice-box and how I set other spaces in the body resonating. In this way I can control not only pitch and volume, but I can also to a degree modify the timbre by altering the range of overtones, also their proportion in combination with the basic tone.

My view is that emotional tone is *carried* by a subtle modification of timbre due to small variations in the range and proportion of overtones, interacting with small variations of pitch and volume. All these variations are the effect of how the voice-box and other structures are being used by control of the breath and resonance. This use is managed in the experiential body, the inner felt body-image, and is directly influenced by our emotional state.

On the one hand this use can be cramped by continuous emotional inhibition. As I said earlier, personal power is the original soul taking charge of its earthly location and our culture is repressive of this process. The voice has direct access to this original being, so the basic timbre of the voice is under social restraint, its full resonance unused, and the emotional tone is constantly subdued.

On the other hand the original uninhibited signature of the voice can be recovered by retraining through various techniques of voice production, especially those involving singing. In charismatic training, the trainee is invited to let the emotional tone of the voice *emerge* out of integrated postural presence. Another way of putting it is to speak from the belly, from the fullness of being here now. Physically, the timbre acquires more resonance, more overtone richness, and emotionally the voice reveals warmth and original value, and becomes empowering for the soul of the listener.

Exercise 1. I have to hand various verses by Blake, Shelley, Wordsworth, Tennyson, Swinburne and other suitable poets. They are stanzas that are lyrical, sonorous, emotionally, imaginatively and spiritually evocative. In small groups people take turns to declaim one stanza with conscious command of timing and especially emotional tone of voice, generating this tone out of the fullness of their original presence. There is a report on the experience from self and then feedback from the others, and perhaps a second or third go to get deeper into the command of tone. End with experience-sharing in the whole group.

Exercise 2. People work in small groups of four or five. Each person takes a turn as facilitator in a short role play practising the use of charismatic emotional tone, as well as timing, in one of these areas: culture-setting statements, making contracts, permission-giving statements, implanting suggestions, handling critical incidents, the exposition of some basic ideas, the deeper point of an exercise, underlining a vital piece of feedback, and so on. Each person chooses whichever of these is most pertinent. A paragraph of delivery is sufficient, then feedback to self, feedback from peers, and several re-runs to take account of feedback and deepen the practice. End with experience-sharing in the whole group.

Phonetic command

I must remind the reader, who may be feeling daunted by this analytic separation of all the many aspects of human expression, and thus wondering however to put it all together in conscious behaviour, that multi-modal functioning is entirely normal to human beings, who love it. It is no problem, but a natural joy, for people to integrate seeing, hearing, smelling, touching, moving, memory, phantasy, reflection, mood, pleasure and intention all in one short sequence of behaviour. In the same way, putting together all the elements of the up-hierarchy of expressive modes is exhilarating and agreeable, the more so because this way of being, suppressed in our culture, releases deep well-springs of personal empowerment.

Phonetic command is the third part of level 2, after timing and tone of voice. It is about the sounds you make in speaking, the pattern of noises you utter. Tune in to a radio programme in a language you do not understand, and listen to the sound of the language just as sound, a stream of patterned noise. Any such language is made up of a relatively small number of phonemes, a phoneme being the smallest segment of sound that can differentiate two words.

The so-called Received Pronunciation of British English has 44 phonemes according to one common analysis, 24 consonant sounds and 20 vowel sounds. Each phoneme may have several variations called allophones: thus the phoneme 'p' sounds different in 'spot' and 'pot', since in the latter the 'p' is pronounced with a puff of breath, but not in the former. And each phoneme has one or more features to do with whether it involves the vocal cords, lips, tongue, nasal passages, and so on. English phonemes are quite distinct chunks of sound, but in some other languages there are phonemes which are distinguished by variations of tone on the same basic sound (Aitchison, 1987).

I mention all this simply to raise the reader's consciousness about an aspect of voice that normally disappears from awareness because we are so preoccupied with what we mean by the sounds we are uttering. But the sound *qua* sound has an impact all of its own. So my proposal is that facilitators let their felt presence in the whole experiential body manifest as the music of vocal sound: the sound they produce then has melodic qualities carried by the tone of voice and the rhythmic timing.

Exercise 1. This exercise is prepared for overnight. Members of the group who speak foreign languages and are familiar with their literature come to the session with well-known lyric poems written in those languages. These poems are read to small groups of those who do not understand the language being used. The listeners listen to the stream of phonemes as melody carried by the tone and rhythm of the speaker's voice, without in any way trying to understand or divine what the poem is about. They then share their experiences of this melody, describing its qualities. Later the speaker gives a brief precis of the poem in English, and this is followed by more discusssion. End with experience-sharing in the whole group.

Exercise 2. People work in groups of four. Each person takes it in turn to practise *glossolalia*, that is, speaking in tongues for a few minutes. This simply means you make up a language: a stream of sounds compounded into 'words' and 'sentences', using a wide range of phonemes which may be entirely imaginary, or which may come from any language you have ever heard. Out of your conscious presence, you voice phonemes as a melody carried by the tone and rhythm of your voice, without in any way bothering about what the sounds mean. You imagine you are doing this in relation to one of your own back-at-work-groups. The listeners first of all give feedback on the qualities of the vocal 'music' produced, then later they discuss what they imagine it could have meant. End with experience-sharing in the whole group.

Exercise 3. People work in groups of four. Everyone takes it in turn to be a facilitator in role play speaking to a back-at-work-group about any chosen significant topic. As facilitator, you become fully present, and speak one paragraph in English, attending fully to the phonemes - letting their melody as a pattern of sound be carried by the tone and rhythm of your voice. Give some feedback to yourself on this melody, and hear feedback from the group; then have a re-run or two to become more at ease in producing agreeable sounds as such while using them to convey meaning. End with experience-sharing in the whole group.

Command of language

In the up-hierarchy of personal empowerment, you let the tone and timing of voice, and music of sound at level 2, shape the command of language at level 3, that is, the choice of words and grammatical structures, the linguistic pattern you use. It is notorious how often facilitators can disempower their own facilitation by riddling their speech with verbal and grammatical detractors. They do this either by subtly undermining themselves, or by putting their listeners down in some implied way. Their choice of words, the forms of speech, show noticeable hints of pleading, apology, fear of rebuff, appeasement, diffidence, insecurity, uncertainty on the one hand; and rebuke, bossiness, condescension, disapproval, dislike, irritation, impatience and suchlike on the other. It is not that any of these things are grossly explicit in the language, but are implicit in the selection of terms and syntax. So the facilitator does not say 'I am too anxious to propose this' but 'I wonder whether perhaps you might mind trying this out'.

All this can be cleaned up from below, so to speak, in using the up-hierarchy. If facilitators are fully present, their experiential body integrating pelvis and lower limbs, belly, heart, larynx and head, and if timing and tone of voice and music of sound are marshalled out of this presence, then a lot of linguistic detractors will simply drop out of their speech. They start talking with their own true inner authority, honouring both themselves and their listeners. To the extent that this does not occur in their training exercises, trainees need to be interrupted as soon as they slip into a verbal or grammatical detractor, and to be invited to run the statement again free of all negativity. Several re-runs may be necessary for some trainees to establish such freedom.

Exercise. People work in groups of four or five. Everyone takes a turn as facilitator in a short role play to practise doing a piece of facilitation they feel anxious about. They use the up-hierarchy model, being grounded in their presence and using charismatic and clock time as appropriate, and allowing all this to shape the language they use. The listeners only attend to the facilitator's language, and interrupt it as soon as any word, phrase or grammatical structure is either self-disempowering or an implied put-down to the recipients. The facilitator attends to being present and restates what was said until all agree it is empowering to both speaker and listener. End with experience-sharing in the whole group.

Command of content of speech

The command of language, just considered, is the basis also at level 3 for taking charge of the content of speech. So the selection and shape of your language, emerging out of all the prior levels of the up-hierarchy, influences *what* you say, the ideas and information, judgments and opinions you put forward. This is where the up-hierarchy and the down-hierarchy meet.

The down-hierarchy is conventional in the culture. It starts at level 4 and works downward by control to level 1. Thus we normally have some purpose in mind in relating to others, let this shape the meaning of what we are going to say, which in turn will select the words and linguistic structures, which will influence the tone, timing and sounds of voice; then posture, gesture, facial expression and relative position will adapt accordingly.

I think that facilitators in their early days rely heavily on the down-hierarchy, having carefully worked out their objectives and their programme - which shape what they say in front of the group. With more experience they disengage from it, keep their goals and plans more distant from their immediate behaviour, and let their presence before the group and their attunement to its energy field shape what they say. But they still have goals and plans in setting up the group, and these will quite properly also exert influence on what they say before the group.

The first meeting place of the two hierarchies is at level three in the content of speech, in what the facilitator is saying. The pre-existent objectives and programme of the facilitator in organizing the workshop - which proceed from the down-hierarchy - will have some general bearing on everything he or she says during it, and from the back of the mind will shape the broad sweep of his or her facilitation.

At the same time what in detail is said at this moment and in this given context in the workshop will be shaped by the up-hierarchy. Most times these immediate, existentially responsive statements will be in accord with the guiding plans of the down-hierarchy. But not always, for sometimes the realities encountered through the use of the up-hierarchy and its grounding attunement to the group life, will mean a discontinuity between what is said and pre-existent plans.

For the most part, through well-established habit, the down-hierarchy can be left to look after itself, so that the facilitator can empower him or herself with conscious use of the up-hierarchy. Thus the content of statements is simplified, gets down to basic ideas and principles, when it emerges from integral presence shaping vocal and verbal command. Innate intelligence shines through, uncluttered by unnecessary parentheses and qualifying clauses. Meanings are informed by the lucid beams of the heart.

As well as content of speech, there is the timing of that content - when it is said; and its direction - to whom it is said, whether to the group as a whole or one or more persons in it. These two vital aspects of speech behaviour go right back to level 2 of the up-hierarchy, and were mentioned as the first part of it.

Exercise. People work in groups of five. Everyone takes a turn as facilitiator in a role play introducing some important piece of theory, or rationale for practice, in your chosen field. Deliver this exposition out of the total up-hierarchy, grounded in your presence, out of which vocal timing (moving between clock and charismatic time), tone and sound, command of language and thus content emerge. After feedback from self and others, take one or two re-runs to deepen the effect. Such re-runs are an important part of any training exercise. End with experience-sharing in the whole group.

Command of purpose

The final stage of the up-hierarchy is to allow the purposes and intentions you have in mind to be shaped by the whole of the preceding levels: your personal presence and rapport with the group, your sense of when to speak and to whom, your timing and tone and sounds of voice, your command of language and of content. As all these are working, emerging one out of the other, they shape and reshape the purposes which lie behind what you are saying. These purposes thus become existentially attuned: flexible, adapted and appropriate to what is happening.

As with the content, ie the meaning, of your speech, the purposes behind it will also be influenced by the down-hierarchy objectives and programme which you bring to the group and which have been expressed in the publicity for it. So level 4 is the second place where the two hierarchies quite properly interact.

This interaction at level 4 is usually tacit and unstated. Often the purposes which arise out of the up-hierarchy will be broadly consonant with your original objectives and programme. At other times, you may be silently modifying and adapting your original objectives and programme to suit the emerging realities of group process. Where there is radical dissonance between the two, renegotiation with the group about its agenda may be required.

The down-hierarchy of facilitator principles

The down-hierarchy starts at level 4, the level of purposes and intentions; and this level controls level 3, the meaning of what is said; and so on. I intend to look only at level 4. There are three main sorts of purposes and intentions involved here.

1. Group objectives. These are the published objectives and the provisional programme of the group. They define the group for prospective applicants to it, and are stated in the prospectus for it.

2. Technical principles. These are the technical facilitator principles which you intend to use in pursuing the published objectives and realizing the programme. *The Facilitators' Handbook* (Heron, 1989) is devoted to what I regard as some of the main ones, such as balancing the use of hierarchy, co-operation and autonomy in managing the dimensions of planning, meaning, confronting, feeling, structuring and valuing.

3. Moral principles. These are overarching ethical norms, of which I believe there are three primary ones, and I review these in the next section.

These three sets of intentions are the guiding lights of the down-hierarchy. Together they provide a kind of continuous sunlight which enables the manifold growths of behaviour within the up-hierarchy to flourish.

Guiding moral principles of facilitation

Every facilitator will have their own explicit or implicit set of such basic principles. I am not talking about intermediate moral principles such as telling the truth, keeping promises and contracts, which I shall take for granted in this discussion, but about the ultimate ones, those which support us in realizing our most cherished values, and on which the intermediate ones themselves rest.

1. The principle of love. I define this, for facilitators, as the commitment to provide conditions within which people can in liberty and co-operation determine and fulfil their own true needs and interests. How to provide these conditions is dealt with by the technical principles mentioned in the previous section and by the group objectives and programme to which they give rise.

2. The principle of impartiality. This means that facilitators are committed to giving everyone in the group equality of consideration. Time and attention are distributed among participants fairly. This does not mean that each participant gets the same time and attention from the facilitator as every other. It means that differences of treatment can be justified by relevant differences between the participants concerned. It is these relevant differences that get equality of consideration: each person's special needs and interests are considered equally. As a result everyone is treated both differently and fairly.

3. The principle of respect for persons. This could also be called the principle of respect for autonomy. It is clearly implicit in the statement of the principle of love, but merits special mention. It means that facilitators are committed to honour the right of every person to make autonomous choices about what they do or do not do in any group, and to be given adequate information about any proposed activity so as to be able to make an informed choice about it.

So here we have three transcendent principles to guide the whole facilitation enterprise. But without the immanent growth of living soul within the up-hierarchy, they become as nothing.

The whole of this chapter by its nature places great emphasis on the empowering presence of the facilitator. This is particularly relevant for intiating students into whole person learning, which is the theme of the next chapter.

3. Holistic learning of a subject

Distinctions within the field

What is holistic, or whole person, learning? The answer depends on what you think a whole person is and how you believe such a being functions. So we are into personality theory: the structure and dynamics of the person. Before getting into all this, let me separate out some of the different sorts of things that holistic learning can include.

The first basic distinction is between holistic learning in the world - in living and in working - and holistic learning in the classroom or group room.

The second main distinction is between learning some ordinary subject or skill by being involved as a whole person, and learning how to become a whole person. The first of these is about educational development - using holistic methods to enhance the learning and teaching of different disciplines; while the second is about personal development. Of course they are not mutually exclusive. If you learn accountancy by a holistic method, you may also gain a little personal development thereby; and if you attend a workshop for your personal development, you will expect to find holistic methods being used. Nevertheless, the difference is clear.

Within each of these two quite different sorts of holistic learning some further important practical distinctions can be made. Let's look at learning a specific subject or skill by being involved as a holistic learner. This can mean that the holistic methods are *inside* the learning: their use is related to mastering the content of the lesson. So you play a game in Spanish as part of the business of learning Spanish. Or it could mean that holistic activities are *alongside* the learning: they are not directly to do with the content of the lesson but are interspersed throughout it to minister to various aspects of the whole person and to keep him or her in good shape for learning. So you dance to music for a few minutes in order to refresh yourself for returning to the business of learning the higher calculus. These alongside goings-on I will refer to as *multi-stranded activities*.

Within holistic methods that are inside the learning, that relate to the content of the lessson, there are those which are organized into some coherent cycle with an underlying rationale, like various versions of the *experiential learning cycle*. There are also those which simply lie side by side without some integrating sequence, and these I will refer to as *multi-stranded learning*.

Among holistic activities not directly to do with the content of the lesson, there are those which directly bear upon the emotional effects of learning. So I may invite students to break off from learning and explore what emotional processes it has been generating within them: they may report these or portray them in sound or movement or a group sculpture. An extension of this is to invite students to take time out from working on a subject to do some emotional work on blocks to learning which they are encountering.

There are three other things that holistic learning of a subject could imply. First, it might mean that in learning the subject, I learn how it directly affects all the different aspects of myself; so in studying astronomy I may learn how it directly affects me spiritually and in other ways. Second, I learn how it is interdependent with a whole range of other subjects which relate to these different aspects of myself; so I may learn how astronomy and theology (or physics, or...) have had a bearing on each other during different epochs. Third, I may learn a main subject always alongside one or more different subjects that are somehow complementary to it.

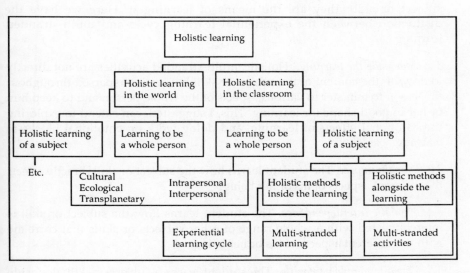

Figure 3.1 *Holistic learning tree*

Learning how to be a whole person, personal development, differentiates itself into several interconnected domains. The first is the intrapersonal, what goes on within the psyche, and this includes attending to what is repressed, what is relatively underdeveloped, and what is entirely undeveloped but not repressed. The second is the interpersonal sphere of face-to-face interactions; the third is the cultural realm of social institutions, their roles, beliefs, norms and values;

the fourth is the ecological zone, interaction with the planetary environment; and the fifth is what I call the transplanetary sphere, more often called transpersonal, the domain of the psychic and the spiritual.

I shall argue in the next chapter that learning to be a whole person involves learning to initiate change in all these interacting areas. These five domains can all involve learning in the classroom or group room, but flow beyond that to be grounded, through action inquiry, in learning in the world.

Below is a brief resumé of the distinctions made so far. The main ones are represented in Figure 3.1.

1. Holistic learning in the world, in living and in working.

2. Holistic learning in the classroom or group room.

3. Holistic learning of a subject or skill. This yields:

3.1. Inside the learning. Holistic methods are used to learn the content of a subject or skill: they are the means of learning it. Here we have the distinction between the experiential learning cycle and multi-stranded learning.

3.2. Alongside the learning. Holistic, multi-stranded activities are not directly to do with the content of the subject or skill but are interspersed throughout the lesson to minister to various aspects of the whole person and to keep him or her in good shape for learning. This, I suggested, can extend to exploring the emotional effects of learning, and doing work on emotional blocks to learning.

3.3. Domain impact. The student learns how the subject or skill directly affects the different aspects of his or her being.

3.4. Domain interdependence. The student learns how the subject or skill is interconnected with a whole range of other subjects or skills that correlate with the different aspects of his or her being.

3.5. Domain complementarity. The student learns a subject or skill alongside one or more other subjects or skills that are complementary to it.

4. Learning how to become a whole person. This involves attention to the intrapersonal, the interpersonal, the cultural, the ecological and the transplanetary domains.

It is my intention in later sections of this chapter to examine 3.1 and 3.2. I discuss 4 as a whole in the next chapter. Before the sections on 3.1, there is an introductory section on holistic and experiential learning, and several about the nature of the whole person.

Holistic learning and experiential learning

I consider that holistic learning is wider than and includes experiential learning in the classroom or group room. The latter is a basic part of the former, but the former raises broader issues about what a whole person is, what aspects of personhood are encompassed. Experiential learning, both in theory and practice in current educational method, involves minimal notions of what a whole person is; whereas holistic learning asks critically what this minimal model leaves out.

Experiential learning theory rests on the philosophic distinction between knowledge by acquaintance, that is, through encounter and meeting and first-hand experience, and knowledge about, or propositional knowledge, which is indirect and does not require any acquaintance with what the propositions give information on. William James (1890) made the distinction clearly and it has continued to be central in philosophy, psychology and educational theory. Kolb (1984) discusses it in detail in his account of experiential learning.

Traditional non-experiential learning is information-bound, all to do with indirect knowledge, knowledge about X, Y or Z. The student listens to lectures to acquire information, reads books and articles for more information, memorizes all this, reflects on it, writes about it in essays and talks about it in tutorials. It is non-stop description, abstraction, ideation, judgment mediated by the written and spoken word. And none of this is grounded in personal experience: the student is locked into a horizontal round of propositional knowledge with no vertical depth in knowledge by acquaintance. The only exceptions are in science subjects which include experimental work in the laboratory.

Experiential learning breaks out of this and makes sure that at some point - *whatever* the subject - the student is involved in direct experiental knowledge, knowledge by acquaintance. This means the student has personal encounter with things, procedures, persons or places that are pertinent to the subject, either literally or symbolically, has inward reactions to them and may take outward action in relation to them. Such encounter, reaction and action may be immediate, by means of some structured experience within the learning situation; or it may be recollected from past personal experience verbally or graphically or by movement or some kind of dramatic portrayal. The student then reflects on this first-hand experience, and by doing so turns it into learning in Dave Boud's phrase (Boud et al, 1985).

Figure 3.2 shows the traditional round of propositional knowledge grounded in experiential knowledge by the use of the experiential learning cycle, applied by exercises interspersed during lectures and tutorials.

Experiential learning is holistic in this significant sense that it integrates within the learning process perception, inner reactions such as emotion and imagination, outward action, and reflection. Its primary dynamic is the movement between the poles of first-hand personal encounter - knowledge by acquaintance - and reflection. Experiential learning is the process of being sensitively tuned in to that encounter and then reflecting on it.

Holistic learning certainly includes this minimal core model of the whole person, but it asks what is left out of this minimal model. What about intuition, psychic and spiritual capacities? How does whole personhood function, and what does this imply for integrated learning? What distinguishes the egoic individual from the whole person and what difference does this distinction make to our understanding of the learning process?

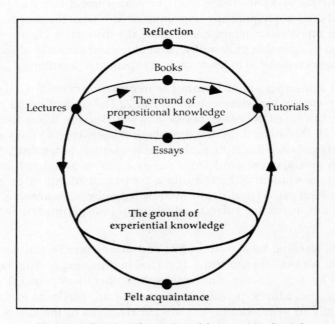

Figure 3.2 *Experiential grounding of the propositional round*

The generally acceptable model of a whole person

The minimal core model which experiential learning people use is itself an extraction from what I call the generally acceptable model of a whole person. This is a workable model for most people in our culture, including psychologists, educators, novelists and the person on the street. It consists of a pool of generally accepted beliefs about what a whole person includes. So we get something like a combination of: perception, memory, imagination, dreaming, thinking, intuition, movement, choice, intention, will, action, sensation, bodily needs (or desires), social needs, emotion (or feeling), interests. Underlying all this is the basic tripartite paradigm of the structure of the person in the Western tradition, which can be traced back to Plato: cognition, conation and affect - thinking, willing and feeling (Allport, 1958; von Eckartsberg, 1981). And in the background there are composite notions like those of person, self, subject, character, disposition and temperament.

While most professionals would probably find everything on the list intellectually acceptable, they will make different sorts of selections from it to suit their different purposes. What is clearly off the generally acceptable list is anything to do with subtle energy and subtle bodies, with extrasensory perception and other psychic abilities, and with transpersonal or spiritual dimensions of the person.

Experiential learning people tend to boil the generally acceptable list down to a minimal core; and I was a bit generous about this core in the previous section. Kolb (1984) has it reduced to feeling, perceiving, thinking and behaving. But he does not define feeling; and emotion, intuition and imagination are excluded from the basic fourfold set. I have given elsewhere (Heron, 1992: 193-197) a detailed critique of Kolb's theory, which is really just a model of experiential learning derived from positivist scientific inquiry: we reflect on experience, generalize from these reflections then test the implications of these generalizations through further active experience.

Others condense experiential learning simply into experience and reflection; or to experience, reflection and action (Henry, 1989). 'Experience' here certainly means perception, and may include other things depending on the experience in question. On the one hand these minimal accounts are convenient for pioneering experiential learning, for getting ideas of it out and about; and for introducing change with a minimum of resistance. On the other hand, their shallowness misses a lot of depths of personhood and potential learning power.

Avant-garde models of the whole person

Our culture being what it is, the generally acceptable account of the whole person is secular and humanist including only biological and psychosocial realities. Avant-garde models go beyond this to include at least a transpersonal, that is, a spiritual, dimension. Thus Jung (1977) works with sensation, feeling, intuition and thinking from the general list, and adds among other archetypes in the collective unconscious the archetype of the self, which is not the ordinary self on the general list but a deep spiritual centre whence proceeds personal integration and transformation. Assagioli (1965) enlarges Jung's selection from the general list to include: desire, sensation, feeling, imagination, intuition, thinking, the (ordinary) self and the will. Then to avoid all the contradictory things Jung bundles into the collective unconscious, he separates the unconscious from the superconscious - which is the home of the transpersonal or higher self. The basic selections of these two theorists are shown in Figure 3.3.

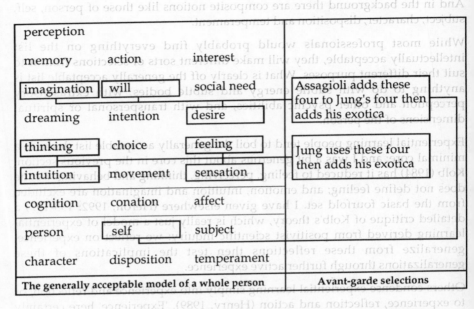

The generally acceptable model of a whole person			Avant-garde selections
perception			
memory	action	interest	
imagination	will	social need	Assagioli adds these four to Jung's four then adds his exotica
dreaming	intention	desire	
thinking	choice	feeling	Jung uses these four then adds his exotica
intuition	movement	sensation	
cognition	conation	affect	
person	self	subject	
character	disposition	temperament	

Figure 3.3 *Avant-garde selections from the generally acceptable model of a whole person*

These are two popular avant-garde models, as also are those derived from Hindu and Buddhist psychology. Swami Rama in the Hindu tradition has a model of the lower mind, *manas,* that integrates sense impressions, interacting with memory, *chitta,* and the separate subject or ego, *ahankar.* Beyond this is the higher intuitive mind, *buddhi,* the locus of wise discrimination and the will. And beyond all this is the Self, *Atman,* the universal witness consciousness, the blissful sheath (Swami Rama et al, 1976).

What is noticeable about these three models, two occidental and one oriental, is that the spiritual dimension of the person, called by all of them the self, is portrayed as different from the various other component parts of the person such as perception, memory, feeling, the will, and is quite different from the everyday self of the general list. It is as if, when you are in an ordinary state of mind, the spiritual self is something you are outside of, or do not know about, or have to find, or meditate or develop into: to get to it you have to go from one psychological place to another of quite a different kind. There is also the implication that you probably need a guide or a guru to help you make the journey.

In the theory of the person I have recently put forward (Heron, 1992) this separation between the spirituality of persons and their everyday psychological functions is done away with. In the next section I give a brief overview of this new theory.

Feeling as the ground of personhood

The distinction between feeling and emotion is quite fundamental, but general confusion abounds. In ordinary usage, 'feeling' is frequently used as a synonym for 'emotion'; it is also used as a synonym for almost all mental states from bodily sensations to subtle intuitions. In more considered usage, philosophers and psychologists have used the word 'feeling' or 'felt' to indicate how we apprehend the world. So William James says that it is 'through feelings we become acquainted with things' (James, 1890, Vol 1: 221); and other philosophers talk about the felt qualities of the world. Kolb (1984) also allocates feeling to the apprehension of concrete experience. But none of these people says what this feeling is that enables us to apprehend things. The word is used, it seems quite aptly, but the meaning is left tacit, a concept shrouded in experiential vagueness.

My view is that while emotion is to do with the fulfilment or frustration of our individual needs and interests in the forms of joy, surprise, anger, grief and so on, feeling is a term I reserve for the capacity of the person to participate in wider unities of being, to indwell what is present through attunement and resonance. Through feeling I become at one with the content of experience, and at the same time know my distinctness from it. This is the domain of empathy, indwelling, participation, presence, resonance, and suchlike (Heron, 1992: 16).

Lawrence Hyde is about the only writer I know who made a clear distinction between the more intense, agitated character of emotion and the creative aspect of feeling by which 'we place ourselves in communion with what we find outside ourselves'. He variously called this empathy, heterocentric evaluation, and identification with the being of things 'in the mode of love' which at the same time enhances our own sense of identity (Hyde, 1955).

Koestler (1964) came close in his valid distinction between self-assertive emotions and participatory emotions, but the notion of feeling was never separated out from the latter. Empathy, from the German *Einfühlung*, feeling into, has been with us for a long while; but its conventional definition implies some special kind of state we need to get into in order to be empathic. In Chapter 2 I suggested how 'empathy' needs to be redefined to rescue it from the idea of self-bound projection.

My point about feeling, as I have defined it, is that it does not have to be discovered: you do not have to make a special psychological journey to find it. Nor does it have to be pulled like a rabbit by meditative magic out of an internal hat. It has only to be noticed as an integral part of everyday living as a distinct being in a multiple world. It is through feeling that we meet our different worlds and engage in resonant transaction with them.

Feeling is a necessay condition of ordinary perception: it attunes us to the manifold of beings which perceptual imagery clothes. We do not know that our imagery is imagery of anything, unless our participative feeling tells us of our distinctness-in-union with what there is. The subject-object split which comes from the conceptual layer in perception - the restless seeing of things as objects of different sorts out there separate from us - may cause us to disattend from the grounding level of feeling our world, to such a degree that it seems to disappear from consciousness. But the felt acquaintance is always necessarily there.

It is feeling which distinguishes between dreams and waking life, because by its nature it is attuned to the differentiation of being into different kinds and levels of particular. So feeling authorizes intuition to understand dream images as portrayals of our inner life, and as distinct from the perceptual world of life awake.

Feeling, in short, enables us to engage with and participate in our various experiential realities, to differentiate them from each other, and to know that we are distinct from any one of them even while being in a unified field with it.

This capacity for feeling is the ground of personhood, is that in which all other psychological functions are latent and out of which they emerge. It is the guiding entelechy of personhood, the formative principle and potential which can be evoked to shape our inner development. It is a profound and immediately accessible spiritual principle, the manifestation of divine life immanent within the psyche. I must refer the reader to *Feeling and Personhood* (Heron, 1992) for further details to enlarge this summary account of a comprehensive theory.

The up-hierarchy model of the whole person

I see the whole person as compounded of four basic psychological modes - the affective, the imaginal, the conceptual and the practical. Each of these is composed of two polar and interdependent functions, a participatory one which makes for unitive interaction with a whole field of being, and an individuating one which makes for experience of individual distinctness. Stating the participatory first and the individuating next, the affective functions are feeling and emotion, the imaginal are intuition and imagery (imagery includes perception, extrasensory perception, memory and imagination), the conceptual are reflection and discrimination, the practical are intention and action. Reflection and discrimination correspond to Piaget's formal operational and pre-operational thinking (Flavell, 1963).

In terms of whole person dynamics, I think there is a basic, ground process going on in which the affective mode as feeling has all the other modes latent within it, and they emerge out of it in what I call an up-hierarchy form.

An up-hierarchy works from below upwards, like a tree with roots, a trunk, branches and fruit. It is not a matter of the higher controlling and ruling the lower, as in a down-hierarchy, but of the higher branching and flowering out of, and bearing the fruit of, the lower.

The basic features of an up-hierarchy are these: what is higher is tacit and latent in what is lower; the lowest level is the formative potential of higher levels; the higher levels emerge out of the lower; there are many different possible forms of emergence; the higher levels are a reduced precipitate of the lower; each level has a relative autonomy within the total system; what is lower grounds, supports and nourishes what is higher.

So the human psyche functions as an up-hierarchy grounded on feeling, the capacity for resonance with being and participative attunement to other beings. Out of the affective mode emerges the imaginal mode, including the imagery of imagination, memory and perception. From the imaginal proceeds the conceptual mode, the domain of thought and language; and this is the basis for the development of the practical mode, the level of intention and action. Figure 3.4 depicts the up-hierarchy with the participatory and individuating modes at each level.

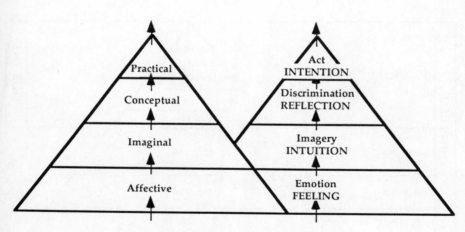

Figure 3.4 *The up-hierarchy of psychological modes*

Especially significant for learning is the view that the patterned fields of the imaginal mode are the source of all subsequent conceptualization. Hence the importance for the student of dwelling in the imaginal mode before explicit conceptual work, in order to make the latter easier and more fruitful. This view has been thoroughly worked out in *Feeling and Personhood* (Heron, 1992) and I must again refer the reader to this for the details.

The ego and the whole person

Another basic distinction I make is between the ego and the whole person. I construe the ego as a relatively separate contraction together, within the practical mode, of the individuating functions of emotion, imagery (mainly perception and memory), discrimination and action. This is illustrated in Figure 3.5. The ego is over-identified with these at the expense of the participative functions of feeling, intuition, reflection and intention and is an activist usurper working in relative dissociation from them. Not absolutely of course, since the ego also uses the participative functions both minimally and exploitatively to serve its own interests.

The ego, which is busy not noticing its ground in participative feeling, identifies with its subjectivity as split off and separate from the objects of the world. Having an ego seems to be a pre-condition of becoming a whole person. And a whole person in terms of this model is one in whom the individuating functions previously contracted into the ego are brought into fully conscious integration with their participative correlates: emotion and feeling, imagery and intuition, discrimination and reflection, action and intention.

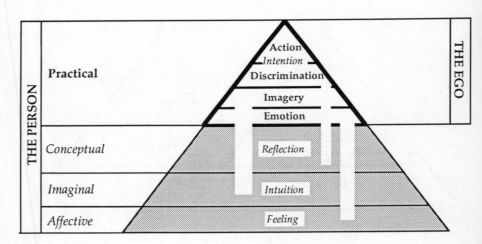

Figure 3.5 *The open ego*

An ego never attains total closure. First it has to feed off the participative functions to some degree even while excluding them and denying them any conscious role. Second there are spontaneous moments of openness when the deeper functions bring their fruits into consciousness, as at times of interpersonal and group communion, contemplation of art and nature, creativity and free experssion, peak experiences. Third there is the option of acquired openness: the ego can learn to create apertures for accessing the deeper reaches of the psyche. Figure 3.5 shows an open ego that has cultivated access to the participatory modes.

Open ego and whole person learning

What all this means for learning is that we need to distinguish between two kinds of holistic learning. There is a more limited sort to do with the ego and which involves mainly the individuating functions of emotion, imagery, discrimination and action; although there will be some shafts going down into the participatory functions of feeling, intuition, reflection and, of course, intention. I will call this open ego learning, a first step in holistic learning.

Then there is the full-blown holistic version, which I call whole person learning and which explicitly integrates in the learning cycle both the individuating and the participatory modes: emotion and feeling, imagery and intuition, discrimination and reflection, intention and action. Open ego and whole person learning, as I use the terms, are two forms of holistic learning within a domain. Whole person learning in this sense is still distinct from learning how to be a whole person - a wider notion which is not domain specific; although it is clear that the two will overlap and the latter will include the former.

Open ego and whole person learning involve experiential learning methods which make sure that at some point the student is involved in felt acquaintance: he or she has personal encounter with things, procedures, persons or places that are pertinent to or symbolic of the subject, and has inner and outer responses to them. Such encounter may occur now within the learning situation through some kind of special exercise; or it may be recollected from past personal experience. The student then reflects on this first-hand experience, and by doing so turns it into learning. I shall give details of open ego and whole person experiential learning cycles in later sections of this chapter.

Closed ego learning

Traditional non-experiential learning is ego-bound, often involving a very closed ego. The learner, moving around between interest, boredom and fear (of falling behind, failing exams, being disapproved of) listens to teachers, reads books, tries to discriminate the presented content, to memorize it and to rehearse it in practice using the written or the spoken word. What is involved here is a closed circuit of the individuating ego functions used in a restricted way: limited emotion, perceptual imagery, memory imagery, intellectual discrimination, and action as writing and speaking.

The learner's emotional base is suppressed and narrow, not in any way attended to by the teacher, and is a disconcerting *ad hoc* mix of conflicting positive and negative emotion. The imagery is reduced: perception is restricted to listening to teachers and looking at books, and memory is confined to the content of these perceived images. Intelligence is only involved in grasping the minimal conceptual geography of the topic; and action is exclusively word-oriented. So the individuating functions themselves, especially emotion, perception and action, are underdeveloped and inadequately integrated. And the propositional knowledge involved in learning has no experiential grounding in direct, felt acquaintance.

Traditional learning starts to shift out of this closed ego format towards a minimal open ego format to the extent that it includes more than mere intellectual discrimination of content and requires the student to engage in active reflection on this content, applying rules (Piaget's concrete operational thinking) or thinking in terms of possible or hypothetical relationships (Piaget's formal operational thinking). You can arrange all subjects in secondary and higher education on a continuum from mere discrimination (the individuating function of the conceptual mode) to advanced reflection (the participatory function of the conceptual mode), depending on the nature of the subject, the level at which it is being taught, and how it is being taught. But there is still the absence of experiential grounding: only science subjects that include experimental work in the laboratory have any base in perception and action.

Traditional methods at most open up the closed ego by sinking a shaft down into the participative mode of reflection. The critical question is how valid an account of the world such reflection can yield when it is developed without other interconnected shafts being sent down into the grounding participatory modes of intuition and feeling, and without integrated development of the individuating functions of emotion, perception and action through the inclusion of experiential activities and exercises.

Primary and secondary cycles

Before going in more detail into open ego learning, it is important to note that there are two different and intimately associated experiential learning cycles, one being included as a phase within the other.

Originally people defined the experiential learning cycle as a movement from a phase of experience to a post-experience phase of reflection. Now it is acknowledged that within the phase of experience itself there is an ongoing learning cycle. 'In any experience there is a natural process taking place within the learner in which what is being taken in is processed, affects the learner and can provide the basis for action' (Boud and Walker, 1992: 167). These authors borrow from Schön (1983) the term reflection-in-action to name this process, and consider that it involves noticing and intervening. In other words, there is a simple feedback loop during experience: you notice what is happening, take account of this in your intervention, notice the outcomes of the intervention, and so on.

This is closely related to Torbert's more elaborate idea of action inquiry, which involves consciousness in the midst of action, a special kind of widened attention that embraces one's intuition or vision of ends, one's reasoned or felt strategy, one's present action, its outcomes and what is going on in the outside world. Such action inquiry not only notices all these, it also identifies and corrects incongruities among them (Torbert, 1991: 219-238).

Boud and Walker (1991, 1992) point out that this reflection-in-action experience is part of a wider learning cycle in which there is preparation for the experience before it begins and digestion of it and reflection on it after it is over. It is important to separate out these two cycles very clearly. The first I call the primary experiential learning cycle; the second and wider cycle, which includes the first as a stage within it, I refer to as the secondary experiential learning cycle. For convenience I will simply use the terms primary cycle and secondary cycle. The primary cycle is entirely internal to and autonomously managed by the learner, once the experience begins. The secondary cycle is managed by the facilitator.

However there are cases where the teacher is generating the learners' experience in the earlier stages of the primary cycle, as in the original form of superlearning: Lozanov's suggestopedia applied to language teaching (Lozanov, 1978; Schuster and Gritton, 1986; Hooper-Hansen, 1992). I outline this kind of superlearning in terms of primary and secondary cycles in a later section of this chapter; and discuss the wider issue of teacher-managed or student-managed experience in the primary cycle of any kind of experiential learning. It is also possible for a whole lesson to be conducted entirely in terms of an extended primary cycle and I also give an illustration of this in another section below. These various options, and the issues involved in choosing between them, simply point to the fact that the whole field is still in early stages of development and awaits a lot more experiential inquiry.

The open ego primary cycle

Experiential exercises used in learning subjects of any kind such as accountancy, chemistry, geography, astronomy can contain within them the open ego primary cycle. This involves mainly emotion, imagery (perception, imagination and memory), discrimination and action. These are all intentionally brought forward and integrated in the learning process. In terms of the up-hierarchy model which I introduced earlier and which is now applied just to these four individuating functions, the ground of the cycle is positive emotional arousal.

This empowers the learner to enjoy a variety of perceptual experiences, imaginatively developed in the exercise. These in turn underwrite and sanction the conceptual discrimination, the propositional structures which are the cognitive rationale of the exercise. And these provide the basis for guiding the action which the learner takes within the exercise.

These, then, are the four basic elements of the open ego primary cycle: positive emotional arousal, varied perceptual experience, conceptual structuring, involvement in action. The exercise starts with initial emotional arousal and perceptual alertness, the conceptual structure guides action, which deepens emotional involvement, which extends perceptual experience, which grounds the conceptual structure, and so on. This is the fundamental order of influence and potency: emotional fulfilment brings life to perceptual experiences, which provide the imaginal warrant for conceptual maps, which give the rationale for action. Once the exercise is under way, the primary ground of its internal learning cycle is emotional arousal. A full discussion of this is given in Heron (1992: 227-238).

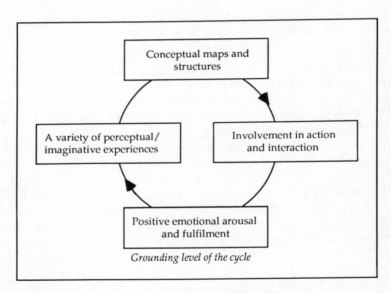

Figure 3.6 *The open ego primary cycle*

The cycle is illustrated in Figure 3.6. Suppose the exercise is that the learners interact with each other within the space of the room to portray the interactive properties of different chemical substances. Emotionally and perceptually alert, the conceptual model guides them into action, which gets them more emotionally involved and fired, to perceive and imagine the configuration of interactions going on between them, which sharpens their discrimination of the conceptual model, which further guides their interactions, and so on.

The internal learning cycle here is the way in which action, perception and conceptual model continuously inform and illumine each other, through their grounding in emotional arousal. At its simplest level this mutual influence is a negative feedback loop: emotionally motivated, I notice that what I perceive is discrepant from the conceptual model, then I modify my actions accordingly.

The participative functions of feeling and intuition are tacitly involved. The learners will have a latent feeling of participating in a common field of experience, of being compresent with each other. They will subliminally and intuitively grasp the whole perceived pattern of their interactions and its consonance or otherwise with the conceptual structures.

So the ego here is open. It is not compulsively activist. It is seeking to learn from aware interflow between emotion, perception and other imagery, conceptual structures and action. The discrimination of conceptual structures will deepen from time to time, depending on the subject, into more elaborate reflection. And the process of the primary cycle, embedded in the secondary, rests on the tacit evocation of feeling and intuition.

The open ego secondary cycle

The secondary cycle is one which the facilitator manages to prepare the learners for the experience beforehand and to enable them to process it afterwards. Whereas the primary cycle follows the basic up-hierarchy converted into a continuous sequence, the secondary one is what elsewhere I have called the reversal cycle (Heron, 1992: 29, 243). This reverses part of the basic cycle and uses the conceptual mode to redirect the imaginal from its habitual set.

The facilitator therefore adopts it when seeking to initiate students who are used to the closed ego cycle of traditional learning into the open ego cycle of experiential learning; and in general, since all egos tend to close again, to inaugurate an open ego attitude in any group. The secondary cycle is emotion-discrimination-imagery-action, while the primary cycle is emotion-imagery-discrimination-action. So it seeks to re-vision the imaginal through prior conceptual structures.

Let us suppose you are discussing the notion of action in the philosophy of mind. One aspect of this topic is the distinction between action and intention, that is, between an action such as raising the hand and what the person concerned meant by that action, what it was intended to achieve. You decide to use an experiential exercise focussed on this theme. You take the learners through the following secondary cycle which includes at stage 4 the exercise as a primary cycle.

Stage 1. Affective. Before launching into the topic of action and intention, you can ask the learners to work in pairs or small groups and take turns to identify positive and negative emotional responses to it simply as a bare topic, to enhance the positive responses and to disattend from the negative at this stage. This honours the individual history which people bring to their learning and alerts them to their initial personal experiential stance within the topic. You may then give some direct or indirect suggestions which affirm the value of this stance and which build up a positive emotional climate for learning.

Stage 2. Conceptual. You now give a brief overview theoretical input about the distinction between action and intention. You discriminate between the two basic concepts and related ones and reflect on their theoretical implications. This leads into informal question and answer and discussion with the whole group.

Stage 3. Imaginal. You then present illustrations, instances, demonstrations, personal experiences, dramatic portrayals, stories, pictures - whatever shows the leading ideas of the theoretical input in living imagery. In the same illustrative and demonstrative way, you describe the experiential exercise you are going to invite everyone to do next.

Stage 4. Practical. You invite everyone now to do an exercise using the four stages of the primary cycle as described earlier - positive emotional arousal, varied perceptual experience, conceptual structuring, involvement in action. So this primary cycle as a whole is within stage 4 of your secondary cycle. Working in pairs, each partner takes it in turn to do the following: repeat the same action three times and each time state out loud a quite different intention for it; then run through the whole of the procedure again using the same action and intentions. Thus one may hold out a hand and say 'I am testing for rain', 'I am waiting for change' and so on.

The actor is alerted to participate fully in this experience through emotional arousal, through different sense perceptions and imagination, through conceptual discrimination and through action; and to be aware of the mutual influence of these on each other. This is the internal learning of the primary cycle; what Boud and Walker (1992), after Schön (1983), call reflection-in-action; and what Torbert (1991) calls action inquiry.

Stage 5. Affective. The first three stages were a preparation for the exercise done in stage 4, and now we start the digestion of it. You ask the learners to go deeper into their personal experiential stance, opened up initially in stage 1. What positive and negative emotions were involved in doing the exercise and also in watching it being done by one's partner? This may mean reliving it through literal, phenomenological description in order to catch the emotional nuances. Invite learners to celebrate, affirm and develop the positive emotional responses; to resolve the negative by dissociation, cognitive reframing, emotional discharge or meditative transmutation. The importance of attending to emotional concomitants of experience was well underlined by Boud et al (1985) in their original paper on promoting reflection in learning.

Resolving negative emotion in these ways presupposes that they are impediments to learning. This may not always be the case. They may be anxieties and disquiets that point to some fundamental flaw in the structure of the exercise, or in the concepts on which it is founded. So it is important to differentiate between negative emotional responses that are blocks to learning and those that indicate ways in which it needs to be reorganized, either practically or conceptually or both together.

Stage 6. Conceptual. Learners are now invited to identify and discuss together all the conceptual issues that arise from the exercise, and to relate these to the topic and the theoretical input of stage 2. So the exercise and the topic are used to inform, illuminate and modify each other. This is the reflection phase of the secondary cycle, and one of its most important.

Learners here are doing one or more of four things: they are cultivating a personal view of the topic, one that honours and manifests at the conceptual, reflective level their personal stance in the world; they are testing for a valid view, one that is consistent with experience; they are developing a coherent view, one that is internally consistent; and they are unfolding a practical view of the topic, one that draws out its implications for personal action and/or social policy.

Reflection can be aided by means of a dialectical interplay with imaginal processes, using graphics, diagrams, spontaneous or directed imagery, movement, mime, sound, music, story, allegory, metaphor, analogy, role play, case-studies, instances, demonstrations, brainstorming, synectics, lateral thinking, and suchlike.

The reflective process of stage 6 can start in the exercise pairs, then develop in groups of four, then continue in the whole group with you the facilitator joining in. There is a sharing, review and discussion in the large group of all the issues that emerged in the pairs and fours. You relate all this where relevant to your original theoretical input, correcting it, amending it, adumbrating it in the light of what people are saying. The process may be developed further in written work. Figure 3.7 shows the facilitator's secondary cycle and embedded in it at stage 4 the students' primary cycle, its internal stages represented by four rotating circles.

The secondary cycle could end here, or it could be carried on to include another primary cycle, as follows.

Stage 7. Imaginal. Learners break into small groups and participate in giving illustrations, instances, demonstrations, personal experiences, dramatic portrayals, stories, pictures - whatever brings out the issues of the conceptual review of stage 6 in living imagery.

Stage 8. Practical. Everyone now goes back into pairs to redesign the experiential exercise in the light of the last two stages, and to take it through the four stages of the primary cycle.

Stage 9. Affective. Repeat and deepen stage 5.

Stage 10. Conceptual. Repeat and deepen stage 6.

This, then, is the open ego secondary cycle, which the facilitator uses to loosen up the closed ego and empower it to maximize learning both within the primary cycle while it is going on, and from it in retrospect after it is over. It encourages students to integrate and enhance awarely in learning all the individuating functions: emotion, perceptual and other imagery, conceptual discrimination, action. In relation to the participatory functions, there is a strong focus in the secondary cycle on reflection, well grounded in personal experience and emotional awareness; intention is widened throughout the secondary cycle; there is a tacit evocation of feeling in the mutuality and compresence of peer learning, and of intuition in the grasp of perceptual patterns and imaginal presentations and their relations with conceptual structures.

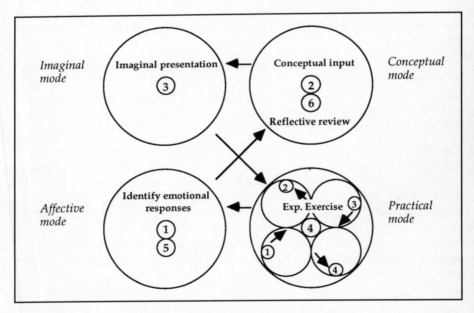

Figure 3.7 *The facilitator's open ego secondary cycle*

In *The Facilitators' Handbook* my account of the experiential learning cycle (Heron, 1989: 64-65) is basically that of a secondary cycle, but it condenses the two cycles into one without identifying the fact. That book does make a clear distinction between the two cycles (Heron, 1989: 127), but did not work out the detail of how they interact. Hence the analysis in this chapter.

Primary and secondary cycles in superlearning

Superlearning is an interesting species of open ego, holistic learning. The essence of superlearning technique, originating in Lozanov's suggestopedia (Lozanov, 1978) and developed more widely as suggestive-accelerative learning (Schuster and Gritton, 1986), is assimilating varied presentations - visual, auditory, kinaesthetic - of the subject matter as a whole at the imaginal level, before analysing and conceptualizing it. This follows a basic precept of the up-hierarchy that full absorption of the imaginal patterning, as such, of material facilitates its subsequent conceptual mastery. Indeed the method accords with the whole of the up-hierarchy model. I use below an example from learning a language, the classic application of the method (Hooper-Hansen, 1992).

I must emphasize that the up-hierarchy model, based on the four psychological modes, which I am using here to categorize the superlearning stages is not one which superlearning people use. Their own rationale derives from a mixture of brain science, research in hypermnesia, suggestion therapy, memory research, behaviourism, learning preferences, and so on. In my terms, however, the method is a form of open ego learning, which involves both a primary and a secondary cycle. The primary cycle is as follows.

Stage 1. Affective. This stage coincides with the second and runs right through it. Students are relaxed while listening to the music described in stage 2: their feeling of attunement within themselves and within their situation is enhanced; and positive emotions are stimulated.

Stage 2. Imaginal. While classical music plays, the teacher reads the foreign language text out loud with dramatic variations of tone and volume related to the music. The students listen and follow the text with a translation and are invited to associate images with what they hear. Then while Baroque music plays, the same text is read in normal voice and the students relax and listen with eyes closed. The text is 1000-1500 words, which is long by conventional standards. At this stage the text is being taken in as a whole, as a presented imaginal pattern, mainly auditory, with visual and associative back-up.

Stage 3. Conceptual. The teacher now goes through the text as students read it aloud, and provides grammatical analysis and explanation of logical connections. This is done in short bursts interspersed with activities and games which apply the analysis, so there is overlap with stage 4.

Stage 4. Practical. This is a phase of much freer autonomous practice, in which students put the language to use in their own way using role plays, games and other activities.

Superlearning emphasizes multiple presentations at the imaginal stage, evoking varied internal imagery, appealing to sight, hearing and the kinaesthetic sense, and involving peripheral as well as central perception, eg through coloured informative posters on the wall. This multi-perceptual approach is carried through into the practical stage of active learning. Superlearning also stresses the grounding importance of the affective stage, emphasizing the value of the following: relaxation; a positive, confident, buoyant emotional climate; co-operation and mutual support among students; the facilitative presence, bearing, voice and behaviour of the teacher.

In taking students into the primary cycle, the teacher also uses a version of the secondary cycle, to encourage students - in my terms - to move from a closed ego state to an open one. Remember this goes affective-conceptual-imaginal-practical, in this case as follows (Schuster and Gritton, 1986).

Stage 1. Affective. The students are invited to go through a series of physical and mental relaxation exercises, to which are attached various suggestions to create a confident, positive emotional attitude to learning.

Stage 2. Conceptual. The teacher gives a conceptual preview of the content of the lesson, an 'advance organizer' (Ausubel, 1960). It may be preceded with a brief outline review of the previous lesson.

Stage 3. Imaginal. This conceptual preview is combined with some acting, demonstrations, stories, songs, playing with objects, by the teacher to illustrate or surround what is being said.

Stage 4. Practical. The teacher now takes the students through all four stages of the primary superlearning cycle, as outlined above.

This whole approach honours all the individuating functions of emotion, perceptual and other imagery, conceptual discrimination, active practice. It makes a strong tacit use of feeling through the use of physical and mental relaxation in opening the secondary cycle, and through the use of music in the primary cycle. Likewise there is evocation of tacit intuition in the latent, indirect conceptual learning that goes on unnoticed during the different presentations in stage 2 of the primary cycle.

Teacher-managed and student-managed learning

The kind of experiential learning which I introduced in the earlier sections on open ego learning I will call BEL, for basic experiential learning; and superlearning or suggestive-accelerative learning I will name SAL. What distinguishes SAL from the earlier BEL, is that the student in SAL is much more passive during the primary cycle. The first three stages are teacher-managed, the teacher is at the focus of the students' auditory experience, and the teacher does the conceptual analysis; only in the fourth stage does the student move from purely inward alertness to external practice. By contrast, in BEL, the primary cycle is entirely student-managed, all four stages being part of an autonomous experiential exercise.

While in both forms the inclusive secondary cycle is teacher-managed, it is noticeably more so in SAL: in its stage 1 the student is passive, being relaxed by the teacher; while in BEL stage 1 the student is independently exploring emotional responses. Also in a later stage of the BEL secondary cycle, the student is engaging in autonomous and considered reflection, in a way which does not occur in the SAL account.

What this brings out is that the use of the experiential learning cycle can involve more or less student autonomy, more or less student activity, and correspondingly less or more teacher direction of the learning process. Clearly students need initiating into open ego holistic learning by the teacher's overall management of the secondary cycle and by the teacher's *design* of the primary cycle. What is not clear is when and how much it is desirable for the teacher to be actively directive *inside* the primary cycle.

Does the early student passivity - apart from inner alertness - in the SAL primary cycle deepen the holism and the learning process, compared with the BEL primary cycle? Is it at the expense of student autonomy and autonomous reflection? And if so, then it can scarcely be properly holistic. Is the early use of autonomy in the BEL primary cycle at the expense of a subtler and deeper holism?

The choice is between a form of experiential learning in which students are mentally and physically relaxed and the teacher generates an experience for them, and a form in which students generate experience for themselves. Which of these two approaches to use in primary cycles may in part be to do with the subject, the level at which it is being taught, the stage reached in the course, and the teacher's flexibility in moving between teacher-directed and student-directed methods.

The two approaches are not mutually exclusive: they can be brought bear upon each other and interfused in various ways. For example, the SAL method can be made more student-centred in the primary cycle. Take the learning a language example given above. After a general briefing about pronunciation, students could work in pairs, taking it in turns to read the foreign text aloud to each other to music in the active and passive concert manner. Then they could work in small groups identifying grammatical structures, and practising them, with the teacher going round as a consultant to help out here and there.

The virtue of this more student-centred approach is that it combines the method of relaxed receptivity and indirect learning with a significant element of autonomy from the outset, putting the method fully in the hands of the students to explore and manage in their own way, and thereby understand more closely how it works for them. Conversely, in the BEL secondary cycle, relaxation, music and suggestion techniques, could be introduced in one or other of the first three stages.

The up-hierarchy and the primary cycle

What I believe to be common to BEL or SAL or any other form of holistic, subject-specific, open ego primary cycle is that implicit within it is the basic up-hierarchy of the individuating functions. The grounding level is a strong affective base in which the learner has a personal stance, that is, a clarified emotional orientation to the topic, is confident and in a state of positive emotional arousal.

This base supports and empowers varied perceptual experiences relevant to the topic - auditory, visual and kinaesthetic - together with their imaginative development. Out of these, when fully absorbed at their own level, emerge the salient intellectual features of the topic within a global view. These in turn are the ground for rehearsal and practice, discussing the material with, and getting feedback from, others.

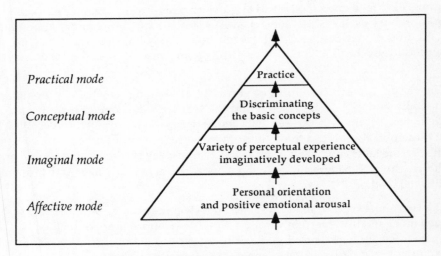

Figure 3.8 *The up-hierarchy of open ego learning*

Figure 3.8 presents these four features in the up-hierarchy model: each is supported by and grounded on those below; the lower are the more basic and the key to the higher. This yields the view that clarified emotional orientation, confidence, and positive emotional arousal are the most important for effective learning of any subject: they constitute its formative potential.

Figure 3.9 echoes Figure 3.6 and shows four features as a continuous cycle, and conveniently tags them as persons, patterns, propositions and practice.

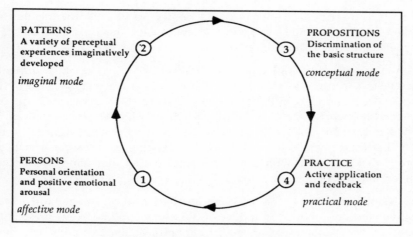

Figure 3.9 *Open ego learning as a cycle*

I mentioned above that a whole lesson could be conducted in terms of an extended primary cycle of this kind. I repeat here the example of this given in my previous book (Heron, 1992: 237-238). It is, of course, suggestive only and could be adapted to any subject matter with a little creative imaginaton and some trial and error improvement through field-testing.

Suppose you are teaching a course on elementary astronomy as part of an adult education programme. The topic for the next two-hour lesson is the solar system. First give your students a brief outline of your holistic strategy, its rationale, and seek their assent to it. This is very important.

Invite the students physically and mentally to relax with eyes closed and listen for a few minutes to 'Jupiter' from Holst's *Planets* suite. Follow this with an affirmation and suggestion about the pleasures, the ease and fluency of learning. Present one or two major myths about the planets, sun and moon. Follow this with the *story* of some key discoveries about the solar system in the history of astronomy. To a background of music expressively recite out loud all the salient data about the solar system you want to include in this lesson: invite students to listen to the music and the sound of your words, with eyes closed, without attending to the conceptual content, and giving any imagery that is evoked free rein. At any point in this five-item sequence give space for spontaneous student-directed comment, question, answer and discussion episodes. Now have a mid-session break.

Follow this with photos and graphics that present the salient data in visual form. Then help students to portray the solar system physically in the room, with very approximate positions, motions and velocities. Let this generate questions, answers and discussion. Next, with music playing very softly, invite students to discriminate the conceptual content of your words together with evoked imagery as you state again the salient data, this time from a different perspective and in a different order.

Follow this with co-operative peer teaching and learning, in which students in pairs take it in turns to share what they now know about the solar system, mythically, historically and factually, by making statements which the other agrees with or corrects, and by asking questions which the other answers or is helped to answer. Encourage them to expand this sharing from the central ground of what interests them; and to make drawings and diagrams as they explore their knowledge with each other. End with a final time for questions, answers and discussion.

This sequence starts at the affective level (relaxation, music and eliciting positive emotion), moves on to the imaginal (myth, story, vocal presentation, visual presentation, kinaesthetic presentation), thence to the conceptual (discrimination of content), and ending with practice (rehearsal of knowledge in co-operative pairs).

The affective base-line of music is used to empower both the vocal presentation of salient data and the later discrimination of its content. The use of music to empower first the imaginal and then the conceptual modes is not to be confused with Lozanov's active and passive concerts (Lozanov, 1978) which are both concerned with the imaginal mode.

This follows the basic cycle closely, but I do not think there is anything especially sacrosanct about always doing so, since additions and variations and inserted sub-cycles will keep the whole thing alive with creative diversity from session to session. What is involved here, after all, is an exploratory project, an experiential inquiry in which you and your students have agreed to chart some of the depths of holism in learning.

The whole person primary cycle

The primary experiential learning cycle involves action inquiry - being conscious of what you are doing and of its outcomes while you are doing it, and altering what you are doing out of this awareness. In open ego learning, this consciousness is mainly involved with emotion, imagery (perception, memory, imagination), conceptual discrimination and action; the participatory modes of feeling and intuition are involved tacitly, and reflection is engaged with explicitly from time to time in the secondary cycle.

In whole person learning, this consciousness is expanded to involve, intentionally, both participatory and individuating functions: feeling and emotion, intuition and imagery, reflection and discrimination, intention and action. So we have here a much more challenging and comprehensive kind of action inquiry. A good example of this at work is in the domain of counsellor training, where the trainee (female) is practising counselling skills with another trainee (male) who is being a real client.

Stage 1. Affective. The trainee practises feeling attuned to the total presence of her client, resonating empathically with his whole way of being. At the same time, the trainee is attending to her own emotions, dissociating from any restimulation or projection. She is managing awarely both feeling and emotion.

Stage 2. Imaginal. The trainee attends to a wide range of perceived images of the client, the whole presented pattern of his behaviour: not simply what he is saying, but how he is saying it in all the different paralinguistic aspects of voice, his body posture, gestures, facial expressions, use of eyes, breathing. At the same time she is taking all this in intuitively as a whole, divining its significance, what revelation of meaning it makes about the client. Here she is consciously engaged with both intuition and imagery at the preverbal level.

Stage 3. Conceptual. The trainee discriminates selectively among all this data, rapidly classifying it, and with quicksilver reflection evolves a working hypothesis about the client's process. This hypothesis will be in implicitly verbal form. The trainee is now involved with reflection and discrimination.

Stage 4. Practice. She converts her hypothesis into a practical intervention based on an underlying therapeutic purpose. She is using intention and action.

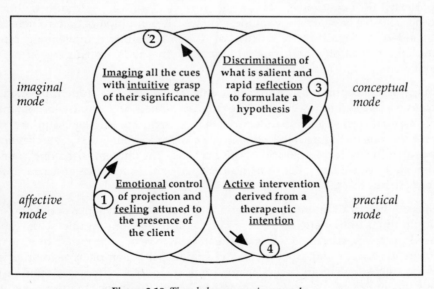

Figure 3.10 *The whole person primary cycle*

This is an inquiry and learning cycle since the client's response, noted in stages 1 and 2, to interventions made in stage 4, can modify hypotheses generated in stage 3, which alter interventions in stage 4, and so on. If this comprehensive kind of action inquiry is generalized to any kind of experiential exercise, then it can be stated as follows.

Stage 1. Affective: emotion and feeling. At the emotional pole of the affective mode, the student surfaces both positive and negative emotions involved in the experiential exercise, harnessing the learning power of positive emotional connections, and resolving negative emotions that obstruct learning. At the feeling pole, the student participates fully in the experience, resonating with and indwelling what is going on. This means a deepened awareness of the normal ground-state of empathic attunement: felt acquaintance with the content of experience is no longer minimal, but raised into a full and enriched consciousness. The student opens to the distinct presences within the experience and feels their immaterial qualities, their unique signatures and gestures of being.

Stage 2. Imaginal: imagery and intuition. While participating in the experience, the student is open to the total configuration of its imagery in perception, memory and imagination; and intuits what patterns of connection there are with configurations of other related experiences, and what the inherent pattern of the experience, its structure and process, is declaring about its domain of being. What is important here is that the student stays at the level of pure intuition of imagery, of its total pattern, its correspondences with other patterns of experience, its ontological declaration, without trying to conceptualize or analyse any of these things. The intuition of pattern here may be aided and realized by the use of drawing, painting, movement, mime, metaphor, analogy and related imaginal methods, during or after the experience.

Stage 3. Conceptual: discrimination and reflection. The student disengages from the felt and intuited experience to discriminate and classify its content in conceptual terms; and to reflect on this content, converting intuitions into propositions including intellectual models and maps, tentative generalizations, possible theoretical implications and suchlike. The student is making connections between deeply felt and intuited personal experience and conceptual frameworks of a general kind.

Stage 4. Practical: intention and action. The student now looks at the practical implications of the reflective phase in general terms, for example, with respect to social policy; considers personal intentions it may be appropriate to adopt for future experience and experimentation, and makes action-plans as appropriate. If the stages are run in cyclic fashion, then stage 4 looks to a re-design of the opening exercise for a second cycle and ends with the actions that lead over into a new felt situation in a second stage 1.

The participative functions of feeling, intuition, reflection and intention subsume their correlative individuating modes. Feeling into the situation encompasses a variety of changing emotional states. Intuiting meaning is exercised in relation to the perceptual and other imagery involved. Reflection presupposes a number of classificatory discriminations having been made. And intention implies, or explicitly formulates, a plan for action.

The significance of the up-hierarchy - affective-imaginal-conceptual-practical - corresponding to the four stages is that the more deeply each stage is entered into, the more it enriches and empowers the subsequent one. Feeling attuned and processing emotions empowers intuitive, imaginal grasp, which is full of latent conceptual content and so enriches the explicit reflective stage, which in turn empowers intention about practical ends.

This account of the whole person primary cycle in terms of the up-hierarchy of the modes is, I believe, rather more substantial than current accounts of experiential learning. In particular it brings to the forefront the grounding importance of conscious feeling as resonant participation in the situation. This feeling of acquaintance, empathy, attunement is *sui generis* and *in situ*. It is an original capacity of the psyche in its own right and is already in place. It is a precondition of all experience, but one which the prevailing world-view disregards in favour of over-hasty intellectual control. The point about stage 1 is not to rush past felt acquaintance in order to get concepts going, but to dwell in it and deepen it on its own account and in its own terms. This provides experiential learning with its immanent spiritual ground.

The corollary of this is the cultivation, in stage 2, of imaginal grasp: the ability to live in patterns of imagery - from perception, memory and imagination - interweaving them, combining and recombining them, until there is an intuition of relevant meaning inherent in the configuration. In pure imaginal meaning conceptual content is inchoate, latent, in seed form: we are dealing with meaning that is intrinsic to imagery, prior to all explicit conceptualization. Again our over-intellectualized culture wants to skirt hastily round all this, and make straight for the conceptual highway. This is paradoxical since the giants of this culture, such as Max Planck and Albert Einstein, were quite clear about the essential role of creative imagination as the ground of intellectual theory-making (Koestler, 1964; Hadamard, 1945).

This whole person primary cycle is therefore counter-cultural in its account of stages 1 and 2. It is even more counter-cultural in proposing that stage 1, the stage of participative feeling, is already a spiritual stage. As the person opens up to embrace this grounding principle of all experience and give it space to expand within ordinary consciousness, however modestly, he or she is directly in touch with a potential for all-embracing unitive awareness. Whole person learning is already a spiritual activity. It does not have to incorporate some transcendental self that is outside the domain of everyday experience. It only needs to acknowledge, affirm and unfold the ever present ground of it. This effectively closes the gap which has hitherto existed between the transpersonal domain and the world of learning.

The whole person secondary cycle

I return to the example of training counsellors used at the start of the preceding section. The trainer uses the secondary cycle to prepare trainees for the primary one and to digest it after it is over. The sequence is similar to the open ego secondary cycle, and includes at stage 4 the primary cycle of counselling practice.

Stage 1. Affective. You, the trainer, invite the trainees to work in pairs or small groups and take turns to work on positive and negative emotional responses to the impending exercise of counselling practice, to process any interpersonal agendas between those who are going to work together, and to affirm and celebrate their participation in the training process. You may give some direct or indirect suggestions which also builds up a positive emotional climate for training. The trainees then ground themselves in mutual attunement, being present with each in the mode of feeling, in some form of interactive meditation or ritual.

Stage 2. Conceptual. You now give a brief theoretical account of the counselling process, identifying the stages of the counsellor primary cycle, the participatory and individuating functions involved in the action inquiry, and whatever else is pertinent at this stage of training. This leads into informal question and answer and discussion with the whole group.

Stage 3. Imaginal. You then present illustrations, instances, demonstrations, personal experiences, dramatic portrayals, stories - whatever shows the leading ideas of the theoretical input in living imagery. In the same illustrative and demonstrative way, you describe the training exercise you are going to invite everyone to do next.

Stage 4. Practical. You invite everyone now to do a practice counselling session using the four stages of the primary cycle, as described earlier in the first part of the previous section. So this primary cycle as a whole is within stage 4 of your secondary cycle. Working in pairs, each partner takes it in turn to be the counsellor for the other as real client.

The counsellor is alerted to participate fully in this experience through feeling and emotion, intuition and imagery, discrimination and reflection, intention and action; and to be aware of the mutual influence of these on each other. This is the internal learning, the action inquiry, of the primary cycle. After trainees end their turn as counsellor, they give themselves feedback on their handling of the four stages of the cycle and receive feedback from their partner who was the client.

Stage 5. Affective. The first three stages were a preparation for the exercise done in stage 4, and now we continue the digestion of it, already launched with the feedback in stage 4. What positive and negative emotions were involved as counsellor and in response to the other as counsellor? These are processed as much as time allows. Positive responses are celebrated; negative ones are worked on either as projections and displacements, or as signs of uneasiness with the process and as cues to what went wrong with it.

Stage 6. Conceptual. Trainees identify and discuss together all the issues that arise from the practice, and relate these to the theoretical model put forward in stage 2. So the practice and the model are used to illuminate each other. This reflective process can start in the training pairs, then develop in groups of four, then continue in the whole group with you the facilitator joining in.

Learners here are doing one or more of four things: they are cultivating a personal view of counselling practice, one that expresses their own stance in life; they are testing for a valid view, one that is consistent with their experience; they are developing a coherent view, one that is internally consistent; and they are unfolding a practical view, one that is effective in and for action. Such reflection can be aided by means of a dialectical interplay with imaginal processes, using graphics, diagrams, spontaneous or directed imagery, movement, mime, sound, music, story, allegory, metaphor, analogy, role play, case-studies, instances, demonstrations, brainstorming, synectics, lateral thinking, and suchlike.

The multi-stranded programme

The open ego and whole person cycles so far considered weld their use of different aspects of the person together into a coherent sequence that has, in my interpretation of them, an underlying theory about the structure and dynamics of the person and of human learning. But it seems to me that any programme of learning must benefit if these aspects are brought to bear upon it, each in a single strand, without these strands being related to each other in some dynamic pattern of learning. In other words they are invoked in a somewhat *ad hoc* way according to mood, intuition, energy level, convenience, logistical factors to do with available space at any given time, and so on.

Each strand is left to find its way across the gap of time or intervening strands to influence every other strand. In the opening section of this chapter I call this multi-stranded learning, if the strands are *inside* the learning process, that is, applied to the subject matter of learning. And I refer to multi-stranded activities if the strands are *alongside* the learning but not applied to its content: they minister to the whole person who takes time out for them in order to enhance subsequent learning.

What is important is that there is a good balance among the strands, a fair representation of each of them, and that all the major ones are thus represented. It is also probably a good thing if there is some kind of balance between those that are inside the learning and those that are alongside it. Such a multi-stranded programme has the virtue of avoiding doctrinaire notions of personality and learning dynamics: in other words it argues that there is some positive influence among the strands but does not insist it must flow this way or that. It only presupposes some view about what the main components of personhood are.

Below is an account of some of the items that might be considered to fall under the main strands according to my theory of the four psychological modes, each with their participatory and individuating functions. Of course there is a lot of overlap, in the sense that many items fall under more than one mode, but I have tried to be true to the main thrust of an item in allocating it to its mode and function. The lists are suggestive rather than exhaustive. They include both inside items and alongside items, and others which can be either inside or alongside. I have decided it would be unnecessarily pedantic to separate out these sorts into different lists.

1. The affective strand: feeling. Physical and mental relaxation; feeling participative attunement and resonance with people, processes and things through immediate experience or through memory; mutual attunement and mutual presence; group attunement to nature; attunement to presences; opening and closing and special purpose rituals; invocations and benedictions; celebration, praise, worship, high prayer; meditation of all kinds; sacred dancing, chanting and singing; inner transmutation exercises; charismatic process groups; sharing peak experiences; making music; listening to music; the use of bells, gongs, candles, incense, robes.

2. The affective strand: emotion. Building self-esteem and affirming self; appreciation and affirmation from and to others; being co-operative and mutually supportive with others; creating a buoyant, confident emotional climate; generating positive emotional associations and connections; creative expression of positive emotion in song, dance, movement, music, art, drama, story-telling, games; listening to music; exploring emotional and interpersonal process underlying the task; identifying, owning and accepting emotional states; redirecting, switching and transmuting emotional states; removing emotional blocks to creativity and learning; clearing projections from and to others; interrupting the displacement and acting out of past distress; catharsis of restimulated past distress.

3. The imaginal strand: intuition and imagery. Many of the following can involve both the presentation and the practice of material: timing, tone, rhythm, inflection, speed, volume, pauses of the voice; pictures, graphics, movement, mime, sound, music; story, allegory, myth; metaphor and analogy; caricature, dramaturgy, role play; cases, instances, demonstrations; associated imagery and resonant experiences; symbolic focus in the group (toy mouse, owl or whatever); insight, intuition, divination; brainstorming, synectics, lateral thinking; guided imagery, active imagination, visualization in all sensory or extrasensory modalities; image-streaming; memory in all sensory modalities;

perception in all sensory modalities; extrasensory perception and exercise of psi capacities; visualization and use of subtle energies.

4. The conceptual strand: reflection and discrimination. Phenomenological description, classification; free or directed association of concepts; divergent thinking; loose conceptual framework; convergent thinking; tight conceptual framework; laws and theories; potentials and possibilities; logical thinking - contradiction, necessary implication; causal thinking - cause and effect; systems thinking - dynamic mutual influence; dipolar thinking - interdependence of polar opposites; contextual thinking - interpretation as a function of culture and history; practical thinking - principles of the form 'to achieve this, do that'; ethical thinking - moral norms and values (Heron, 1985).

5. The practical strand: intention and action. Purposes and intentions; long-term and short-term goals; means and ends; options and outcomes; action-plans and programmes; exercise of the will; action; direction of the execution (Assagioli, 1973); discussion methods, choice and decision-making methods; body-work and bodily exercises; breath-work and breathing exercises; games; structured exercises of all kinds; technical skills; aesthetic skills; interpersonal skills; political and organizational skills; ecological and economic skills; psychomotor skills.

The supposition in using any of these items as part of a multi-stranded programme is that some of them will be inside the learning and some of them will be alongside the learning. This gives great freedom to the facilitator and to the participants to explore the use of holistic learning without being tied down by any strict format. The facilitator will need to make some clear initial decisions about the use of hierarchy, co-operation and autonomy in planning such a programme, as discussed in Chapter 1.

In practice in this kind of programme some form of the experiential learning cycle will also frequently be used, if only in the basic format that after any structured kind of exercise related to the content of the learning, students will want and need to give feedback and to process and review what went on.

4. Learning to be a whole person

In the opening section of Chapter 3, I distinguished between learning some subject matter or skill by holistic methods, and learning how to be a whole person. The former, I said, is to do with educational development, which may have some incidental personal development by-products; the latter is to do with personal development full-on, and will involve holistic methods. I wish now to look at this latter business, of learning how to be a whole person. So we enter the world of personal growth, interpersonal skills, social change, ecological awareness, and transpersonal unfoldment.

The self-creating person

The distinction between holistic learning of a subject and learning to be a whole person is the difference between dipping down into the deeper reaches of yourself in order to learn something, and dipping down into deeper reaches of yourself in order to integrate with them. In the former you open the ego up only while learning and only for the purposes of learning; in the latter you open the ego up so that it will remain so for living and chunks of it may be permanently dissolved.

There are, of course, cases where the two things start to merge. Thus some forms of whole person learning within a domain, such as the counselling training used as an example in the previous chapter, will themselves involve basic elements of personal development applicable in life generally.

In terms of the up-hierarchy model of the person introduced in the previous chapter, learning to be a whole person means integrating the individuating functions of emotion, imagery, discrimination and action with the participatory ones of feeling, intuition, reflection and intention, within the self, in face-to-face relation with others, and in concern for wider cultural and ecological issues. The person is embarked on the phase of self-creating (Heron, 1992: 59-61), of becoming intentional about liberation from the trauma of childhood and the constraints of social conditioning, and about releasing the deep potential of the affective and imaginal nature.

He or she is dealing with old emotional fixations in the basement of the psyche, developing integrated functions on the ground floor in interpersonal behaviour and in promoting cultural and ecological change, and acquiring a psychic, subtle and spiritual perspective on the upper floors - which begins the process of self-transfiguration (Heron, 1992: 61-63).

The whole person as a web of relations

If holistic learning of a subject raises issues of what a whole person is, even more so does learning how to be a whole person. General systems theory, increasingly evoked as a post-positivist paradigm (Bateson, 1979; Capra, 1983; de Vries, 1981; Jantsch, 1980; Koestler, 1964, 1978; Laszlo, 1972), commends itself as a framework for thinking about personhood.

In systems thinking, a whole person is to be defined not simply in terms of the integration of all internal parts, but also in terms of the integration with wider wholes of which the person is her or himself part. In other words a whole person is to be defined in terms of both internal and external relationships. The inner nexus and the outer nexus are interdependent in a total web of relations. Here is my current model of this web.

1. Intrapersonal. At the core of the web is the internal structure and dynamics of the person: the four psychological modes - affective, imaginal, conceptual and practical - each with their polar participatory and individuating functions, related in terms of the up-hierarchy.

2. Interpersonal. Intrapersonal, internal relations are set within the nexus of face-to-face interpersonal relations: what goes on within me is interdependent with past and current encounters with others.

3. Cultural. Interpersonal relations are embedded within the nexus of a sub-culture and a culture. By a culture I mean a language, and social structures with their established roles, practices and rituals, their pervasive values, norms and beliefs; and a sub-culture is one component part of all this.

4. Ecological. A culture is framed within the nexus of the ecological domain. 'Ecology' in its original usage in biology refers to the involvement of the organism with its environment. I use it here to mean the connections between a whole culture and its environment. So this includes its economic relations in the use of natural resources in industry and agriculture, and the various sorts of interactions involved in town and country planning, communication and transport systems, wildlife conservation, climate control, waste disposal and so on. It also covers all those relations of a passive kind, where the culture is simply receptive to what the planetary environment delivers, such as night and day, the seasons of the year, its basic geography and endowments and so on.

5. Transplanetary. The ecological domain and all the previously listed parts of the web are set within the nexus of the transplanetary field. By this I mean two things, the realm of the psychic and the subtle; and the unitive field of universal consciousness. The term often used here, and I have used it myself elsewhere (Heron, 1992), is 'transpersonal'. But if we are defining the personal as necessarily included within the interpersonal, the cultural and the ecological, then the term 'transplanetary' seems more apposite.

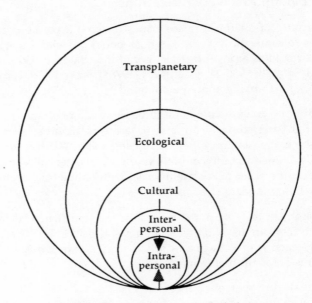

Figure 4.1 *The whole person as a web of relations*

The total web can be conceived as a set of circles sharing a common peripheral point, with the intrapersonal circle the smallest and the transplanetary the largest, as in Figure 4.1. Each circle is influenced by its relations with every other, the inner circles being more affected by everything else than the outer circles. To take just two adjacent circles, the planetary environment has more effect on human culture than the other way round. Each circle has a relative autonomy: it has a degree of independence from the influence on it of all the other circles. The relative autonomy and self-regulation of the planet as a biological structure has been put forward as the Gaia hypothesis (Lovelock, 1987).

In Figure 4.1 the circles are all grounded in a common point. This is to symbolize that through the intrapersonal ground of feeling, as I have defined it in the previous chapter, the person has the capacity to participate in all the circles and differentiate between them.

Given the logical structure of this model, you could argue that the latent capacity for autonomy is greater for each successive inner circle simply because it has a more dense web of relations to transcend and on which it can exert some counter-influence. So the individual person has the greatest *potential* for autonomous functioning. There is also the pragmatic reason that unless individual persons have the maximal capacity for independent action, they are going to be permanently overwhelmed by the sway of all the encircling forces.

What the model propounds, therefore, is that while individuals are most subject to all the combined effects of the web, they also have the greatest potential capacity to change it. There is a two-way influence: a down-hierarchy from the circumference to the centre, and an up-hierarchy from the centre to the circumference. While the down-hierarchy is always actual in the lives of persons, their role as the ground of the up-hierarchy can be in various states from the potential to the less or more actualized. This is represented by the arrows in Figure 4.1

A working definition of a whole person

What this model brings out for the definition of a whole person is that to be one means that the complete web is involved: a whole person is in a set of whole interpersonal relations in a whole culture in a whole planetary environment integrated with its transplanetary field. In each case here, whole means developing in orchestrated harmony. Since the web is not in this state, but is torn and damaged, such a definition is unrealistic and inapplicable. So we have to choose one that is more workable.

The next closest definition, it would seem, is that whole persons are those who have exercised their relative autonomy to integrate their intrapersonal life - so far as this is possible within a total web that is limited - and who are involved in a combined interpersonal, cultural (socio-structural), ecological and transplanetary change programme of activities and commitments. In other words since they cannot now be in a whole and healed web, they are seeking to bring one about. Whole persons are internally together change-agents of a rather comprehensive kind. They are defined in terms both of psychological integration and of holistic initiatives in the other four interdependent spheres. Whole personhood is faced with a paradox: until all spheres are healed and hale it cannot be achieved, and it can only be achieved by making them so.

What is clear on a systems view is that the purely individualistic account of personhood is at an end. A person is a vast web of inner and outer relations, and all our respective webs overlap and interweave.

The agenda for learning to be a whole person

The agenda for learning to be a whole person extends now from personal, intrapsychic growth, through interpersonal skills, to organizational and political change and development, thence to environmental development, and transplanetary (transpersonal) development. This agenda might involve developing the underdeveloped or the undeveloped aspects or both. What is either underdeveloped or undeveloped furls out to cover all the other four spheres beyond the immediate intrapersonal one. We can now no longer present the personal growth agenda as one which is separated off from these wider issues; and vice versa.

Because of the breadth of the agenda, learning to be a whole person is necessarily a piecemeal enterprise. We cannot do it all in one workshop or one course, or in one phase of life-experience, but will bring the underdeveloped and the undeveloped things on bit by bit, here and there. Nor do I believe we can be dogmatic about which of the five spheres to start in, as long as it is acknowledged that whichever one we begin with all the others will sooner or later have a claim upon our attention; and as long as the presenter of any one of them is regularly pointing to its connections with the others. This is an age in which different people do indeed start in every one of the five spheres, and progressively add others to it on an idiosyncratic path of development. And this is no doubt as it should be in our multifarious universe.

My own preference is to give first place to the intrapersonal sphere on the grounds that working on hidden emotional distress will reduce its tendency unawarely and compulsively to distort behaviour in other spheres. More positively by unfolding our capacity for feeling, for resonant attunement with and participation in our world, we find the ground within for integrating all the spheres and for grasping their interdependence. Here are just some of the items within each sphere which may be on the total agenda. I refer to several other publications where I have explored them in depth.

1. Intrapersonal. Healing the wounded child within, and discharging its repressed distress; using the complementary method of transmuting distress; being able to exercise aware control of emotion of all kinds; unfolding the expressive power of positive emotion (Heron, 1982a, 1990); cultivating the grounding capacity for feeling participation in the world and the wider universe as a distinct being within it; releasing the depths and power of the imaginal mind, including extrasensory competence; integrating thinking and action with the depths of the affective and imaginal being (Heron, 1992).

2. Interpersonal. Relating to others free of hidden projection and unaware displacement; managing harmoniously the boundaries between togetherness and separation, communality and privacy; moving flexibly between the relations of co-operating, following, leading, and being autonomous; balancing giving and receiving; balancing supportive care with supportive confrontation; having a wide range of informal intervention skills - prescriptive, informative, confronting, cathartic, catalytic and supportive (Heron, 1990); having a wide range of group process, group discussion and group decision-making skills.

3. Cultural. Being clear about the sources and processes of social oppression in its various forms; education as social transformation not cultural transmission; social empowerment through consciousness-raising and community action; revisioning of their situation by oppressed minorities; mutual support networks of various special interest groups; transforming social structures from within by political initiatives, persuasion, organizational development methods, and techniques of soft revolution; balancing hierarchy, co-operation and autonomy in organizations run as learning centres (Heron, 1989); challenging rigid social structures from without by direct nonviolent action; creating innovative social practices in different spheres of life; devising rituals to enhance the meaning of important occasions in life; decentralization and federalism; creating alternative institutions, social structures, nuclear societies and self-generating, self-transforming cultures.

4. Ecological. Green consumerism - biodegradable products, natural cosmetics, organic additive-free foods, lead-free petrol, recycled paper, artificial furs, vegetarian diet; recycling of paper, glass bottles, cans, rags, plastic, cars, and ultimately all natural resources; ethical investment in ecologically clean companies; ecologically sound control of pollution and waste; population control; reduction of animal husbandry; promotion of animal rights, reduction of animal vivisection; preservation of rare species, wildlife, wilderness areas, the countryside, forests, topsoil, irreplaceable resources; planting trees; self-regulating eco-economics, abandonment of undifferentiated economic growth; soft technology, solar energy and energy from other renewable resources; industrial democracy, work co-operatives, overlap of worker, owner, manager roles; work flexibility, ownwork, work portfolios; reduction of defence budgets; reduction of expropriation of profits by multinational companies from the third world (Gowan et al, 1979; Porritt and Winner, 1988).

5. Transplanetary. Development of subtle energies and faculties in human beings; use of subtle energies within nature; co-operation with creative forces, powers and presences in the subtle worlds; consciousness-raising about the influence of the deceased; development of unitive awareness in and with the world; resonance with universal consciousness; evocation of the immanent divine; invocation of the transcendent divine (Heron, 1988b, 1992).

Locations, domains and cycles

The diverse items given in the previous section mean that learning to be a whole person involves at least six different locations: within the psyche; everyday face-to-face social interactions; the classroom or group room; the work-place as change arena (see Chapters 5 and 6); community consciousness-raising, support or action groups of various kinds (see Chapters 6, 7 and 8); the wider multi-dimensional universe. The first is in the intrapersonal domain, the second in the interpersonal, the third, fourth and fifth in the cultural/ecological domains; the sixth in the transplanetary domain.

The distinction between learning in the world and in the classroom made at the outset of Chapter 3 is no longer tenable in any rigid way: the two here stream in and out of each other. The primary experiential learning cycle, with its four stages, introduced in Chapter 3 in relation to holistic learning of a subject, is taken out into the world and applied in living, in each of the domains of the whole person nexus. This is shown in Figure 4.2. Learning to be a whole person goes out to the world and through the world, transfiguring it with spirit.

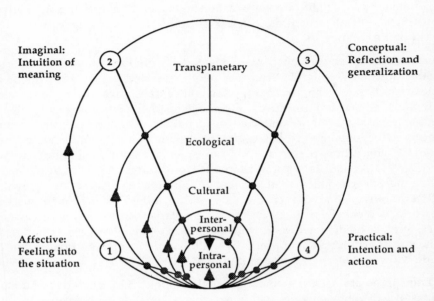

Figure 4.2 *The whole person web of relations and the experiential learning cycle*

A self-generating culture

What this entails is individual and co-operative action inquiry within a learning culture. Each person in the everday process of his or her personal and professional life is adopting a form of action inquiry, a primary experiential learning cycle. For Torbert (1991) this means extended consciousness-in-action, widening attention to encompass your vision of goals, your strategies to achieve them, your current actions and their outcomes, and what is going on in the world around. It also means noticing and amending, either through action or internal revision or both, incongruities between these components of your lived inquiry.

In my model of the whole person primary cycle, this consciousness-in-action involves, intentionally, both participatory and individuating functions: feeling and emotion, intuition and imagery, reflection and discrimination, intention and action. So you feel into and participate fully in the immediate situation, notice and manage your emotional responses to it, grasp intuitively the significance of the total perceived pattern of what is going on, discriminate its salient features and reflect rapidly on the issues involved, formulate a relevant intention and act upon it. Again these several elements influence and revise each other in cyclic feedback fashion, resolving dissonance, deepening learning and worthwhile living.

In the whole person web of relations, such action inquiry will have its idiosyncratic private strands, its shared and face-to-face strands with people at home and at work, and its more collective strands within a learning organization and a wider learning culture, all of which take account of ecological and transplanetary concerns. It will involve primary cycles of living and learning; with time out in secondary cycles for review, reflection and goal setting. The totality of all this I call a self-generating culture, a society whose members are in a continuous process of learning and development, and whose forms are consciously adopted, periodically reviewed and altered in the light of experience and deeper vision (Heron, 1987: 165-170).

Torbert presents a similar notion. For him, personal action inquiry 'aims at creating communities of inquiry within communities of social practice'. It exhibits 'transforming power' which 'operates through peer cultures, liberating structures, and timely actions. Cultures are truly peer-like, structures are liberating, and actions are timely, if they simultaneously promote widening inquiry about what is the appropriate mission, strategy, and practice for the given person or organization or nation, while accomplishing established objectives in an increasingly efficient, effective and self-legitimizing manner' (Torbert, 1991: 100).

A self-generating culture is thus one whose forms its members continually recreate through cycles of experiential learning and inquiry. It has several strands.

1. Decision-making. Persons need to explore forms of decision-making, so that in their different sorts of association they can balance deciding by oneself, deciding co-operatively with others, and deciding for others. These forms need to be adopted intentionally, subject to periodic review, with an accepted procedure for changing them. I assume this same conscious learning process, without stating it, for all the points that follow.

2. Association. Persons need to explore different forms of association in daily living and working, so that they can find ways of balancing the claims of being and doing things alone, together with others, or beside others.

3. Economics. Persons need to explore forms of economic arrangement so that they can awarely choose different ways of distributing and combining the roles of owner, manager and worker; and choose different forms of income and wealth distribution.

4. Ecology. Persons need to explore ways of caring for their planetary environment, sustaining and enhancing its dynamic eco-system.

5. Education. Persons need to explore forms of providing for children and young people of all ages: how they are to be cared for, raised and educated, and by whom. They need to explore forms of education and training for the personal and professional development of adults, and which include techniques for dealing with individual and social overload of emotional distress.

6. Intimacy. Persons need to explore forms of intimacy, that is, ways of giving social form to their sexuality. The point about this form - whether it is open bonding, closed bonding, celibate bonding, serial bonding, or any other - is that it is chosen awarely in the presence of others, that there is a support network for it, and that there is an acknowledged social process for changing the form.

7. Conflict. Persons need to explore forms of conflict resolution: different ways of dealing with hostility and tension, irrational outbursts, irreconcilable opinions, broken agreements, confusion of purpose, and so on. They need to devise such forms, have them in readiness, and learn to use them when they are relevant.

8. Rituals. Persons need to explore and improvise rituals, special events, holidays and feast-days, to celebrate, mark, or mourn the great recurring themes of their individual, social and planetary lives: birth, coming of age, relationships, graduations, visits, arrivals and departures, beginnings and endings, the seasons, solar and lunar cycles, death, and so on. They need to explore, receive and improvise rituals: to foster their inward, occult and spiritual development; to interact with the unseen worlds, their powers and presences; and in communion to attune to the presence within and beyond creation.

Whole person values

In the model of the five spheres and their learning agendas, there is implicit a set of values. This set is encoded in the notion of a harmonious system in which larger wholes include smaller wholes, or to state it in complementary language, smaller parts are subsumed in larger parts. Parts at the same level co-operate in relations of mutual interchange and reciprocal action. Wider wholes have influence over the parts they contain. Single parts have a relative autonomy of function both in relation to co-operative relations with their peers and in relation to influence from wider wholes. Single parts thus have influence on their peers and on their wider wholes. The total system exhibits autonomy, co-operation, down-hierarchy and up-hierarchy. These are its four forms of power, control, effect, guidance, direction or influence: self-influence, peer-influence, down-influence and up-influence. They are illustrated in Figure 4.3.

This model derives as I have said from general systems theory. But it is also influenced by the notion of organic unity in aesthetic theory (Beardsley, 1958), by logical analysis of the concept of a whole (Nagel, 1963), and by theory of value (Perry, 1954). It seems to point to some archetypal, federal concept that crops up in many domains of inquiry. I have stated it in the form that makes most sense to me. But all stated versions contain some or all of the basic elements I have included.

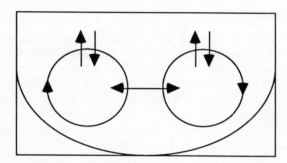

Figure 4.3 *The four forms of influence: self-, peer-, down- and up-*

Translated into a combined account of human values and human rights, it comes out something like the following. As stated, this version extends only through the intrapersonal, the interpersonal and the cultural spheres.

1. Human integration is intrinsically worthwhile. Each person has a right to unfold and harmonize all different aspects of him or herself.

2. Human self-determination is intrinsically worthwhile. Each person has a right to determine and fulfil in his or her own way his or her basic needs and interests.

3. Human co-operation is intrinsically worthwhile. Persons have a right to meet together to determine and fulfil together their shared needs and interests.

4. Human up-hierarchy is intrinsically worthwhile. Persons have a right to participate in decisions that serve their welfare, whether in the home, the community, the workplace, the larger society or the world.

5. Human down-hierarchy is intrinsically worthwhile. Persons have a right to make decisions that serve the welfare of others whether in the home, the community, the workplace, the larger society or the world.

6. Human conflict-resolution is intrinsically worthwhile. Persons have a right to co-operate in resolving (a) conflicts between personal needs and interests and shared needs and interests, and (b) up-hierarchy and down-hierarchy claims.

7. Human diversity in unity is intrinsically worthwhile. Persons have a right to meet together to celebrate and affirm their different states, needs, interests and claims.

The values of self-determination and co-operation are importantly interdependent. There is no real co-operation going on unless it is between self-determining people; and self-determination is achieved and exercised in co-operative relations with others similarly engaged. Nevertheless they do not coincide. There is an element of relative independence in each: some valid self-determination is non co-operative; and some co-operation compromises everyone's self-determination.

The values of up-hierarchy and down-hierarchy are likewise interdependent. There is no valid down-hierarchy, decision-making for others, unless up-hierarchy participation has authorized it; and up-hierarchy participation presupposes there is some valid down-hierarchy to participate in. But again there is relative independence: some valid up-hierarchy influence can be to oppose the down-hierarchy, or create an alternative to it; and some valid down-hierarchy decisions can properly be made - as in a sudden and unforeseen contingency - without any authorization to make them.

Many modern accounts of values and rights omit the down-hierarchy item. This seems to me to be a serious mistake. It is probably omitted because it has been and is being so badly misused in terms of oppression and exploitation. But these abuses do not serve 'the welfare of others' and so fall outside my definition. A worthwhile down-hierarchy principle affirms the right of people to exercise responsibility, care and consideration for others.

The main thing that characterizes down-hierarchy decisions in the social sphere is social size. With a small face-to-face group, co-operative and consensus decision-making can be used. With a large federation of smaller social groups, federal decision-makers will be authorized by the groups to decide some things without consultation, and to canvas and consult the groups on other issues. But even with these latter issues, crisis and rapid change may call for non-consultative decisions.

If societies move to more and more decentralization, so that strong up-hierarchy influence can be exercised by people in their local communities on many aspects of their living and working, then there will be a correlative need for federal bodies up to the global level, where the down-hierarchy influence will be strong. Global decision-makers, authorized through up-hierarchies to make certain sorts of decisions non-consultatively, will have awesome responsibility and power.

In everyday life, the down-hierarchy principle is inalienable. You may be in one of many positions in which you have a right and a duty to make decisions that serve others, and this without consulting them, because they are too traumatized, too young or too ill or too old or too ignorant and unaware, too far away, because there is no time to do so, and so on.

The principle also applies in the sphere of special expertise. This is an area where it has been much abused, in the sense that in many professions the experts could consult the laity a great deal more before making their decisions. Even so, there can come a point when lay persons defer because they are out of their depth and have to say 'You decide for me'.

The up-hierarchy principle is strongest in the intrapersonal sphere, within the psyche, where it can have unimpeded reign in ordering the relations between the psychological modes and functions; next in interpersonal, face-to-face groups where each person can have a lot of say in shaping any corporate decisions that are made. In the wider social groupings of the cultural sphere, the principle moves from strong to weak along a spectrum from the very local and decentralized to the very global and federal.

In the total ecological sphere, even in ecologically competent societies, up-hierarchy influence is much less than in the cultural sphere since so many environmental parameters are immune to its influence - night and day, planetary geography, and so on. In the transplanetary sphere of subtle worlds, hardly anyone knows what is going on in them in any reliable way in terms of decisions being taken by presences brooding over earthly affairs and so intentional up-hierarchy influence is virtually zero.

This may change in the future, when we may enter an era of two-world politics, in which people in this world seek representation on those decision-making councils in the other which preside over human societies. In the present climate of physical world chauvinism, this notion will appear fanciful and extravagant. For acknowledgement of the subtle dimension of experience, see Grof (1988).

Conversely, if the thesis of physical and subtle worlds is correct, then at present the non-consultative down-hierarchy principle is strongest at the transplanetary level: the Creator/Creatrix and his/her hierarchies do not confer with human beings about the design of their psychological and physical endowments, their physical and psychic environment, or the social possibilities which these delimit. As I say, this one day may become different. The down-hierarchy principle is strong but accessible for human influence in the ecological sphere, and becomes progressively less dominant through the cultural and the interpersonal and is weakest in the intrapersonal.

Many moralistic and psychological systems for organizing the intrapersonal sphere have noted (a) that the down-hierarchy controlling principle is innately weak and (b) that chaotic and primitive sorts of up-hierarchy influences seem to be at work such as desires and passions and selfish and irrational impulses. This has led them to try to install down-hierarchy forms of psychological control with high intellect (Plato) or rational conscience (Bishop Butler) or the reality-oriented ego (Freud) taking charge of the whole, with one or two subordinates helping out.

This has not worked very well, largely in my belief-system because the intrapersonal sphere is innately an up-hierarchy zone. Properly understood, chaotic up-hierarchies are the precursors to deeper, more enriching and more creative ones that can harmonize with those of other persons, and with the outer spheres on the great web of personhood. I have already outlined my version of such a creative and worthwhile up-hierarchy within the person.

5. Personal development in the workplace

Group room and workplace learning

In the last chapter I proposed a model of the whole person in terms of a nexus of internal and external relations from the intrapersonal through the interpersonal, the cultural, to the ecological and transplanetary. I also suggested that learning to be a whole person, personal development, can no longer be confined to the intrapersonal and interpersonal spheres in the group room, but also streams out, through personal and collective action inquiry, into the cultural, the ecological and the transplanetary realms. In this chapter I wish to follow this stream and explore personal development as a process that goes on in the workplace. If the workplace becomes an arena for personal development in my extended sense, then the work leader or manager becomes a facilitator of such work-based development. How does such a facilitator-manager go about it?

In answering this question I shall adopt the same basic model as that presented in *The Facilitators' Handbook* (Heron, 1989). This was devised entirely for facilitators of experiential learning groups: it was conceived as a manual - both conceptual and practical - for those whose job it is to direct and elicit whole person learning in personal growth groups, interactive skills groups, management training groups, staff development groups and the like. But the learning process which flows from the group room to the workplace falls within the same fundamental modes and dimensions. The principles remain the same, only the way they are defined and used is noticeably modified by the new context; and one dimension is renamed.

So I shall apply the model to the business of managing a team that has a task in the world. The main focus is on occupational tasks, although the model can be applied to leadership of recreational or social tasks.

There is an important difference between personal development in the group room and personal development in the workplace. In the group room the primary goal is personal development, and any effect out there in the world is usually left for each person to work out later. A task team's goal is to have an effect in the world, and personal development in the workplace is susbsumed within that end. In the group room, change in the world is secondary and a later consequence of learning in the group; in the workplace, personal development within the team is an essential component of changing things in the world, and is thus more grounded and fulfilling.

Before applying the model, I shall take a look at the organizational revolution currently afoot that makes the idea of the manager as the facilitator of personal development in the workplace plausible and relevant.

The organizational revolution

Doctrines of human rights are marching inexorably forward, advancing from the political to the economic arena: in particular what in the previous chapter I called the up-hierarchy principle - the doctrine that every human being has a right to participate in decisions that affect his or her needs, interests, and activities. This right for workers to participate in managerial decision-making is reinforced by a right for increased self-determination at the site of work. And this in turn is enhanced by the spread of educational and psychological values of personal fulfilment and expression.

At the same time there is a pronounced tendency in the modern world toward large organizations. If these become monolithic, hierarchical bureaucracies, then three interrelated problems set in: unmanageable complexity, relative inefficiency and human alienation among staff. So the organizational revolution stems from the need for manageable complexity and for efficiency; as well as from needs for participation, self-determination and self-realization for persons at work. And it is made more feasible in format by rapid advances in automation, computers, artificial intelligence and the whole range of new information and communication technology.

Some features of this revolution (Handy, 1985; Garratt, 1987) are as follows:

1. Democratic representation. Employees have formal representation at board level, and so participate democratically in central decision-making.

2. Autonomous work groups. Employees are in small self-managing, peer supervision groups, organizing their own work and quality control.

3. Co-ownership and co-management. The traditional distinction between owner, manager and worker starts to break down. Workers and managers become co-owners with other shareholders. Management is diversified and its functions shared by all staff in different ways and at different levels. At one extreme of this tendency is the full-blown co-operative whose workers are the primary shareholders, and who hire their managers on contract.

4. Consent cultures. Organizations inform, confer with and consult their staff, rather than control them.

5. Flexible management. The manager is one who can move awarely and appropriately between the three modes of making decisions *for* people, making decisions *with* people, and delegating decision-making *to* people.

6. Project teamwork. Management shifts from classical unity of command at the upper reaches of a hierarchical pyramid, to project teams of specialists. These teams are co-operative and horizontally structured, with overlapping and variable functions, and last only as long as the task requires. Adhocracies.

7. The learning organization. Organizations see themselves as learning systems, in which human resource development is continuously applied within them to make them self-transforming.

8. The shift from wages to fees. This means paying people fees for work done independently to a certain standard, rather than paying wages for time spent under managerial control. Work becomes professionalized.

9. Contracting and networking. The large organization contracts-out work to a network of independent professionals - individuals and teams.

10. Federalism and devolution. Large organizations shift to the federal model, with a central secretariat serving and supporting a network of many small human-sized and semi-autonomous enterprises.

No. 5, flexible management, is the special theme of this chapter, which seeks to provide a comprehensive repertoire for the manager who wants to facilitate personal development in the workplace in a way that enhances the team fulfilling its task. This means moving between the three modes of decision-making on each of the main dimensions of management.

Flexibility of management style is fundamental to the concept of the manager as personal development facilitator: one who can direct the team, can negotiate with the team, can delegate power to the team, and can switch between these three modes as appropriate. What is fundamentally involved is the reconciliation of the personal autonomy of the worker with the authority of the manager, the claims of the organization and benefit to the world.

The manager, the team and the task

The manager may be formally appointed to the role by an organization, formally elected in some democratic way by team members or their representatives; self-appointed to recruit and lead a team; given the role by custom, convention and social practice; or informally selected.

By a team I mean more than just a loose association of people co-operating together. It has at least enough structure for someone in it to have a managerial role that is acknowledged by its members; and for it to have a clearly defined task in the world, also acknowledged by its members. So a team is partly defined in terms of management and task. I shall use the term 'teamwork' to mean 'a team with a leader engaged upon its task'. More formally and fully stated, a team can be defined in terms of four interacting features:

1. Persons and tools. The team consists of suitably skilled people with the equipment they need to do the work.

2. Goals and plan. The team has a task, consisting of work objectives and a programme of work.

3. Roles and rules. The team has a defined social structure of roles and rules which specify members' working functions and interrelations.

4. Power and control. The team has a system of power and control, whereby decisions are made. I return to these features of a team later on.

The team may be an organization, or may be employed by one - working within it, or on contract for it. The team may be appointed or elected. It may be an independent group with a self-appointed task; it may be an informal impromptu task group. But it is by definition a group of people with an accepted manager who are working together on a project that engages them with the world.

The notion of a team is a relative one. It is system-oriented: it can be a whole including lesser wholes. An organization is a large team containing sub-teams, its various departments; each department is a medium-size team containing further smaller sub-teams; there are selective teams, such as department heads; and so on. I leave to the reader to choose what part of a total system their use of the word 'team' refers to, and to adapt the meaning of my text accordingly.

By the task I mean an undertaking to act in a certain way in the social and physical world to fulfil a stated purpose. The term can be used for occupational, social, and recreational enterprises. It can be extended to the social fringe to include, for example, a team which conceives its task as the management of the ceremonial life of a religious community.

All this makes the phrase 'the manager of a team with a task' have a very wide potential application. It can refer to anyone who is seen by himself and a group to be guiding the group to do something in the world. But, as I have already said, I shall be writing here about the world of work, of occupational tasks. There are basically four kinds of occupational task (which I deal with later):

1. Renewal tasks. They deal with servicing equipment, in-house education and training, relaxation, recreation.

2. Development tasks. They create new forms and content for the three other kinds of task, and develop work in new directions.

3. Production tasks. They are productive of goods or services.

4. Crisis tasks. They deal with emergencies, unexpected contingencies or catastrophes.

Dimensions and modes of management

I now give an overview of the dimensions and modes of management. By the *dimensions* of management I mean six different basic issues in relation to which the manager can influence the team in fulfilling its task. In my model, there are the six main parameters for managing any working group. By the *modes* of management I mean three different ways the leader can make decisions within each of these dimensions: by direction, by negotiation, or by delegation.

The six dimensions of management

1. The operating dimension. This is the operational aspect of management: it is to do with guiding implementation of the plan, with methods of supervising work in the field, with ways of structuring the activities in the workplace. The management issue is: How can the work-in-progress of the team be supervised and managed?

2. The planning dimension. This is the power aspect of management: it is to do with decision-making about (i) the objectives, the work goals of the team, and (ii) an integrated programme to realize those goals. The management issue here is: How can decisions about the objectives and work-plan of the team be made?

3. The confronting dimension. The confronting aspect of management is to do with raising team members' consciousness about distorted behaviour that is disturbing job satisfaction, work effectiveness or both together. The management issue is: How shall the team's consciousness be raised about these matters?

4. The meaning dimension. The meaning aspect of management is to do with five interrelated aspects of the meaning of work: (i) the knowledge required to do the task; (ii) the learning acquired in doing it; (iii) knowledge of the effects of doing it; (iv) work being meaningful by virtue of its nature and how it is put together as an intelligent whole; and (v) work being meaningful because of its wider moral and social significance in the world. The management issue here is: How shall all five kinds of meaning be given to and found in the task of the team?

5. The valuing dimension. This is the intuitive, moral aspect of management: it is to do with creating a work culture with core values, with an ethos of respect for persons and for their planet, one in which team members can be genuine, fulfilling their rights, duties and interests as human beings in their ecological context. The management issue is: How can a work culture with core values, and a climate of respect and integrity, be created?

6. The feeling dimension. This is the concern for the affective aspect of management: (i) managing the fulfilment of human needs and interests in and through work - job satisfaction; (ii) dealing with emotions and interpersonal relationships within the team where these are involved in or influence the task; (iii) attending to empathy, attunement, participation, resonance, rapport of people in their total setting. The management issue is: How shall job satisfaction, emotions, relationships and resonance within teamwork be handled?

These six dimensions interweave and overlap, being mutually supportive of each other. Nevertheless, I hold that each one has an independent identity and cannot be reduced without remainder to any one or more of the other five. They are all needed, together, in conscious use, for effective management. The manager as facilitator of personal development at work is one who can move with flexible response among them.

From the point of view of a culture of personal development in the workplace, the grounding, underpinning dimension is that of feeling. Supported by it, at the next level are valuing and meaning and occasionally confronting. At the third level, based on the levels below and shaped by the requirements of the outside world, are planning and operating. This is depicted in Figure 5.1, which also shows correlations between the six dimensions and the psychological modes of the up-hierarchy discussed in Chapter 3.

	THE WORLD	
Level 3	Operating Planning	*Practical mode*
Level 2	Confronting Meaning Valuing	*Conceptual mode* *Imaginal mode*
Level 1	Feeling	*Affective mode*
	PERSONS	

Figure 5.1 *The six dimensions between persons and the world*

The How question stated under each dimension raises an issue in two parts. One part is about what method or strategy will be put forward in any decision made. The other part is about who will make that decision - the manager alone, the manager and the team together, or the team alone: this takes us into the three *modes* of management, given in the next section.

The three modes of management

Each of the six dimensions of management can be handled by the manager in three different modes. Each mode provides a different answer to the question as to who should make decisions on strategies for each dimension. Hence I call the modes decision-modes.

1. The hierarchical mode. Here you, the manager, direct the work of the team, and decide issues for the team: you lead from the front by thinking and choosing on behalf of the team. You supervise on-site work by direction, decide on the programme of work, confront resistances, give meaning to the work, manage satisfaction in the group, and choose values for and inspire them in the work force. As manager you exercise power over the team.

2. The co-operative mode. Here you share your authority and decide issues with the team: you collaborate and consult with team members, prompting and enabling them to participate in the management process. You supervise on-site work with the team through negotiation; you negotiate the programme of work; you initiate conjoint consciousness-raising about resistances; you confer about the meaning of work; you consult about satisfaction and feelings; you confer about the values of the team and collaborate in creating a climate of mutual respect. You lead from within the team, generating, sustaining and guiding a working collective. As manager you share power with the team.

3. The autonomous mode. Here you delegate authority to the team members; decisions on issues are made by the team. You affirm the autonomy of its members, do not manage things for them, or with them, but give them freedom to manage things their own way, without any intervention. With your support, but without direction from or collaboration with you, they use peer supervision on-site, evolve their programme of work, find ways of confronting their resistances, give meaning to their work, manage their needs and feelings, elect their own values and create a climate of peer respect. The team is a self-directed peer group. As manager you affirm the power that is exercised autonomously by the team.

Working in the autonomous mode, delegating power, is a good measure of the manager as facilitator of personal development at work. It does not mean the abdication of responsibility, the dereliction of duty which is involved in pushing on to others what one cannot be bothered to do oneself. It is not oppressive and exploitatory. Nor is it patronizing and parental. It is the subtle art of creating conditions within which people can exercise self-determination both to fulfil themselves and to meet the requirements of the task.

These three modes deal with the politics of the workplace, with the exercise of power in managing the six dimensions of teamwork. They are about who has control and influence. Who makes the decisions about what team members do, and when and how they do it: the manager alone, the manager and team together, the team alone? The three modes of direction, negotiation and delegation are in a higher order political dimension that runs through all the basic six, as shown in Figure 5.2.

The effective manager - as facilitator of personal development in the workplace - is someone who can use all three modes on each of the six dimensions as and when appropriate; and is flexible in moving from mode to mode and dimension to dimension - as and when appropriate. This is no doubt a counsel of perfection. But it broadens the imagination of the manager to keep the total 18-part grid of options in the back of the mind.

	Operating	Planning	Confronting	Meaning	Valuing	Feeling
Hierarchy: direction						
Co-operation: negotiation						
Autonomy: delegation						

Figure 5.2 *Dimensions and modes of management*

Too much hierarchical direction, and team members become dependent and unenterprising, or hostile and resistant, or overtly conformist and covertly deviant. They wane in self-direction - the core of all effective work. Too much negotiation may undermine clear direction by the manager, and self-determination by the team. Too much delegation by the manager and autonomy for the team may result in confusion of purpose.

Each team, depending on its personnel, its task and organizational context, will require a different balance of these three modes. And any given team may need this balance to change at different phases of its work. At the outset, perhaps, clear hierarchical management; in the middle phase, co-operative and shared management; and in the later phases, complete delegation and team autonomy. But there is no rule here: it all depends on the team, the task and the context.

The modes can include each other. A hierarchical manager who hires a team can subsume elements of co-operation and autonomy in his or her style, deciding unilaterally what job the team will do, deciding co-operatively with them how long it will take, and delegating to them all decisions about methods and ways of working.

Conversely, an independent team decides on its task, then hires a manager and contracts with him or her the different respects in which his or her leadership style will be hierarchical, co-operative and autonomous. The team's autonomy contains the other modes. So the modes can be interwoven in many different ways.

To illustrate this, we can apply the three modes to each of the following: the goals of the task, the programme of work to realize goals, and the methods of working, as in Figure 5.3.

	Task Goals	Task Programme	Task Methods
Hierarchy	Manager alone	Manager alone	Manager alone
Co-operation	Manager with team	Manager with team	Manager with team
Autonomy	Team alone	Team alone	Team alone

Figure 5.3 *Configurations of power in the workplace*

This gives 21 ways of combining hierarchy, co-operation and autonomy in decision-making about the task: 21 configurations of power in the workplace. At one extreme, the manager alone decides on the goals, the programme, the methods. At the other extreme, the team alone decides all these things, so it has no manager.

In between are 19 ways of distributing power between manager and team with respect to the goals, the programme and the method of work - some more obviously relevant than others. Nor does this take into account possible combinations within each column, for different sub-goals, programme parts, etc.

Task and process

Three of the dimensions deal primarily, but not exclusively, with the task of the team: the operating, planning and meaning dimensions. Operating is about ways of managing on-site work, planning is about the goals and programme of work, meaning about the knowledge needed for and generated by work.

The three other dimensions - confronting, feeling and valuing - deal primarily, but not exclusively, with the process in the team. By process I mean what is going on within people and between people as the task proceeds. While powerfully influenced by the task, process can always be described in relative independence of it.

The confronting dimension is about the resistances, blocks, avoidances, distorted behaviours within the team. The feeling dimension is about the satisfactions and emotions arising out of the work and the working conditions, and about the quality of interpersonal relationships. The valuing dimension is about core values and norms, workers' rights - whether these are being respected, and whether the team can function with integrity.

One important part of the meaning dimension, the inherent meaningfulness of work, is closely related to job satisfaction on the feeling dimension.

The three modes too are about a central aspect of process: the business of making the decisions. Decision-making also can be described - in terms of who and how - without any reference to what aspects of the task are being decided about. If we put all this on the grid, with the application of each of the modes being the application of a process on either a task or a process dimension - as these have been just been defined - then we get the allocation as in Figure 5.4, where P means process and T means task.

	Operating	Planning	Confronting	Meaning	Valuing	Feeling
Hierarchy	PT	PT	PP	PT	PP	PP
Co-operation	PT	PT	PP	PT	PP	PP
Autonomy	PT	PT	PP	PT	PP	PP

Figure 5.4 *Task and process related to the dimensions and modes*

What this brings out is that, from the point of view of management style, the comprehensive leader needs three times as much process awareness and proficiency as task competence. Within the grid, the term P for process occurs 27 times, T for task 9 times.

Eighteen basic management options

I now present an overview of the dimensions and modes combined into 18 basic options for the team manager. For convenience I have numbered each option as in figure 5.5. Do not be misled below by the simplified statement of each option. The different modes within each dimension are not mutually exclusive: they can all be used on the same task, at different times, and for different aspects of the given dimension.

	Operating	Planning	Confronting	Meaning	Valuing	Feeling
Hierarchy	1	4	7	10	13	16
Co-operation	2	5	8	11	14	17
Autonomy	3	6	9	12	15	18

Figure 5.5 *Dimensions and modes of management (numbered)*

1. The operating dimension: hierarchical mode. You manage on-site work for the team. You are directive in supervising your team at the workface: you tell people what to do, and intervene in what they do.

2. The operating dimension: co-operative mode. You supervise on-site work with the team. You negotiate with team members on how they do their work: supervision is collaborative, decisions at the workface involve you and them.

3. The operating dimension: autonomous mode. You delegate the supervision of on-site work to the team. The team becomes an autonomous work group, managing their own day-to-day tasks, practising self-directed peer supervision.

4. The planning dimension: hierarchical mode. You determine work goals for the team and do the planning to realize them, deciding unilaterally on the content and time-scale of the work programme.

5. The planning dimension: co-operative mode. You determine goals and plan the work programme with the team: you are committed to negotiate, to take into account and seek agreement with the views of team members in devising content and the time-scale of the plan.

6. The planning dimension: autonomous mode. You delegate goal-setting and the planning of the work programme to the team: you are getting out of the way, leaving the team to work out its own schedule.

7. The confronting dimension: hierarchical mode. You interrupt distorted behaviour, raise consciousness about its effects and its source, and do this directly for team members - in such a way that those concerned may awarely alter their behaviour.

8. The confronting dimension: co-operative mode. You work with the team to raise consciousness about distorted behaviour: you prompt, invite, ask, compare and share views with them about the behaviour, its effects and its source; consciousness-raising is collaborative.

9. The confronting dimension: autonomous mode. You hand over consciousness-raising about distorted behaviour to the team: you create a climate of support and trust within the workplace, so that the challenge to distorted behaviour occurs independently within the team, through self and peer confrontation.

10. The meaning dimension: hierarchical mode. You make sense of what is going on for the team: you are the source of all relevant knowledge about the job, and of giving meaning to work events, making work meaningful.

11. The meaning dimension: co-operative mode. You invite team members to participate with you in generating understanding: you collaborate with them in generating all relevant knowledge about the job, and in giving meaning to work events, making work meaningful. You give your view as one among their views and co-operate in making sense.

12. The meaning dimension: autonomous mode. You delegate knowledge and data gathering, interpretation, feedback, reflection and review to the team; making sense of what is going on, giving work meaning, is autonomous, entirely generated by the team.

13. The valuing dimension: hierarchical mode. You create the core values for the culture for the team, the ethos of respect for persons and their planet. You take strong initiatives to care for team members.

14. The valuing dimension: co-operative mode. You collaborate with the team in developing the core values of its culture. You create a community of mutual respect, through dialogue about what the team stands for and about how it will manifest this.

15. The valuing dimension: autonomous mode. You delegate to the team the creation of its own core values and culture. You respect team members as self-governing persons who, in relation with each other, establish their own primary ethos and norms.

16. The feeling dimension: hierarchical mode. You take charge of the emotional being of the team for the team, decide what will maximize fulfilment and satisfaction at work, and implement it. You think for team members, judging what ways of managing emotions will suit them and their working relations best. You set up basic rapport and resonance.

17. The feeling dimension: co-operative mode. You negotiate with the team ways of maximizing fulfilment and satisfaction at work. You manage the emotional life of the team collaboratively, discussing with members different ways of handling working relations, and of creating underlying attunement and resonance.

18. The feeling dimension: autonomous mode. You delegate to the team ways of maximizing fulfilment and satisfaction at work. You give the team space for the process of managing its own emotional and interpersonal life, and for generating resonance in its own way.

Personal development in the workplace

The manager as facilitator of personal development in the workplace selects from among these 18 options to create a managerial style that progressively moves toward more delegation to team members: increased self and peer determination at the site of work in managing quality and productivity; increased participation in central policy-making and planning; increased self and peer regulation and discipline in handling wayward behaviour; increased self and peer initiative in generating knowledge and understanding through work, and in giving meaning to work; increased self and peer attention to job satisfaction, whole person satisfaction within the conditions of work, and interpersonal relations; increased self and peer commitment to generate and sustain core values. The operative word here is 'increased': it does not mean total or absolute, but just increased delegation compared with the traditional norm of over-control from above. It will need balancing with negotiation and direction.

An important point is that the more these self and peer processes increase, the greater the decentralization of work. And that also means, as I discussed earlier, that there will need to be a correlative increase in federal co-ordinating centres, and therefore an increase at these centres in certain kinds of down-hierarchy direction. This developmental polarity is the challenge of the future. What underlies it are the basic whole person values outlined at the end of the previous chapter: the values of integrated self-determination, co-operation with peers, up-hierarchy participation in decision-making, and down-hierarchy exercise of responsibility. The more self and peer determination at the decentralized end of the scale, the more down-hierarchy responsibility at the federal end of it. Personal development at the workplace means that everyone there has an experience of these polar values, bridged by the up-hierarchy, interacting to enhance everyone's personal development and the work being done.

The increases in self and peer processes are not brought about by immediate massive delegation, but by a graduated developmental sequence in which direction, negotiation and delegation are progressively mixed in varying proportions. Such a programme may typically start with a strong element of direction and move toward a significant amount of negotiation and delegation. But such generalization is misleading. It is impossible to give any detailed account of this sort of development, since it is entirely situational. It depends on the nature of the team: what its task is - whether renewal, development, production or crisis, the kind of organizational or professional culture in which it is embedded, what stage in its history has been reached, who its members are, their education and experience, their level of personal and professional development.

Transforming power

The manager who is using direction, negotiation and delegation (hierarchy, co-operation and autonomy) in varying proportions in order to empower personal development in the workplace - in the form of increased self and peer determination - is exercising a higher-order kind of transforming power. It is equivalent to the redefinition of political authority in the learning environment which I discussed in Chapter 1. Through his or her own action inquiry in using the three decision-modes, the manager is seeking to create a team whose members are also engaged in self and peer action inquiry, and who see their work as an arena for experiential learning.

I borrow the term 'transforming power' from Torbert for whom it means seeking to empower others through the creation of 'liberating structures' within organizations. Such structures are ones in which there is a sense of shared purpose among subordinates, an increasing self-direction among subordinates, and a commitment to generate quality work among subordinates. They are structures which simultaneously cultivate among members both quality improvement and other aspects of productivity on the one hand and action inquiry and personal development on the other. 'If liberating structures succeed organizational members will increasingly take executive responsibility, will increasingly treat one another as peers, and will increasingly create their own liberating structures' (Torbert, 1991: 100).

For Torbert, the leader exercising transforming power of this kind essentially invites mutuality and participation in power; but will also use what he calls unilateral, diplomatic and logistical power to further this end. There is therefore a strategic irony in the whole business. This is similar to my proposal that the manager use hierarchy, co-operation and autonomy in flexible and imaginative ways in order eventually to elicit more self and peer determination among team members along the six dimensions of management.

The team dynamic

By the team dynamic I mean the combined configuration of mental, emotional and practical energies in the team at any given time; and the changes which this configuration undergoes at different phases in the team's existence, in response to several interacting factors. These influential factors include: the structure of the team; the tasks of the team; the motives of its members; critical issues to do with the team's organizational and social contexts; ideology; the authority of the manager; and the vision of the manager. To have a consistent feel for and overview of the team dynamic is a central key for the manager as facilitator of personal development and liberating structures in the workplace. The rest of this chapter outlines my theory of such an overview. So the whole of what follows is an extended map of the field within which transforming power is exercised. It is offered as a cartography that may facilitate strategic thinking for the facilitator of team members' personal development in the workplace.

The structure of the team

As I wrote earlier, any team, as the concept is used in this book, can be defined in terms of four interacting features. Each feature itself consists of two interdependent factors.

1. Persons and tools. The term 'persons' refers to the particular people through whom the team is made manifest, its present personnel, their skills and level of competence; and 'tools' to the equipment and technology which they use on the job. Without trained persons and their tools or technology there is no actual team. In general, the sort of persons recruited to join the team will influence its process, as will the kind of technology used by it. Technology can have a very strong influence indeed on how the team functions as a social structure. Thus the new information and communication technologies are capable of supporting radically new organizational forms - which allow much more autonomy at the workface. It is the very development of these technologies that makes more and more possible the kind of flexible management style which I am advocating.

2. Goals and a plan. The term 'goals' refers to the team's working objectives and 'plan' to the programme which enables these objectives to be realized. Together they define the task of the team: they state what it is about. The basic different kinds of task are analysed in the next section. The task of a team is a primary determinant of its dynamic - or should be.

3. Roles and rules. The team has a more or less evident social structure which specifies members' working functions and interrelations. The term 'roles' refers to the different positions in the social structure of the team, and 'rules' to their job-descriptions and responsibilities. This social structure is independent of whoever happens to be occupying the roles at any given time. And within one organization, the same person may have different roles in several teams.

4. Power and control. The team has a system whereby management decisions are made. It has a *de facto* command procedure - which may not always correspond with how that procedure is defined on paper. The procedure may be different for longer-term policy and planning decisions as against day-to-day executive decisions. But the team is always managed by one or more persons somehow. The term 'power' refers to who is doing the managerial decision-making, and 'control' to what procedures they use in doing it.

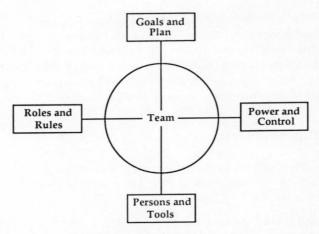

Figure 5.6 *The four features of a team*

The first two of these are interdependent: workers and their tools must be suited to the task and vice versa. The second two are also interdependent: the social structure will define the allocation of power and control, and those in power can redefine the social structure of roles and rules. In a rational world, the last two should be grounded on the first two: the structure of roles and rules and allocation of power and control should be devised so that they are best suited to the people involved, their equipment and the nature of the task.

The four features are shown in Figure 5.6. The duality within each arm of this figure can generate tension and requires internal accommodation. The four arms themselves are in dynamic tension with each other: a creative compromise between mutual support and mutual antagonism. They also provide a template for a set of manifold correlations, tendencies to alienation and distortion, that illumine the dynamic of any team. I consider these affinities first of all from the standpoint of the different sorts of task.

The tasks of the team

Earlier, I outlined four very general yet very relevant ways of classifying the tasks of a team. Every team will be involved with each of these four kinds of task at different times in its history. At the same time each team will focus strongly on one kind of task. The four kinds are shown in Figure 5.7.

1. Renewal tasks. The work of the team is to service, replace or update its equipment, and introduce new technologies; to undertake education and training, professional and personal development; to relax, refresh and re-create itself; to gestate for the next phase of activity. All sorts of technical service teams, staff development and training teams, welfare teams, recreational facility teams specialize in renewal tasks.

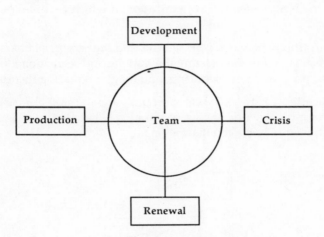

Figure 5.7 *The four tasks of a team*

2. Development tasks. The team's work is to innovate, to develop work in new directions and by new methods, and to solve problems to make this possible. A secondary but important aspect of such work is to solve the problems that arise in closing down old directions and old methods - the innovation of closure. Research and development teams specialize here.

3. Production tasks. The work of the team is to sustain some form of production, in a steady state, or in phases of expansion or contraction. The vast majority of teams specialize in tasks of this sort - in two basic categories:

3.1. Tasks productive of goods, together with the diverse tasks that support the producers, such as producing and distributing raw materials, marketing and distributing the goods.

3.2. Tasks productive of services, together with the diverse tasks that support the servers and market their services.

4. Crisis tasks. The job of the team is to deal with sudden emergencies disturbances, dangers, difficulties and critical events. Examples of specialist teams here are: fire-fighting teams, police teams, medical teams, military teams; and all kinds of trouble-shooting teams.

Renewal and development tasks have a bearing upon each other: unless people are well educated and trained and in good physical and mental shape, they cannot develop their work in new directions; and through development work they deepen their learning and their motivation. Renewal and development are also best seen as the ground and support of production and crisis tasks, otherwise goods and services, and the solution of problems in delivering them, fall by the wayside of social and technological change. An organization that is a developing one is also a learning organization in which personal development can take place.

There is some affinity between *renewal* tasks and the *persons and tools* feature of a team: renewal is to do with meeting the training and recreational needs of the persons in the team, and with servicing, updating or replacing their tools.

There is some affinity between *development* tasks and the *goals and plan* feature of a team: development work means re-thinking what the team is seeking to achieve and how it is going about achieving it.

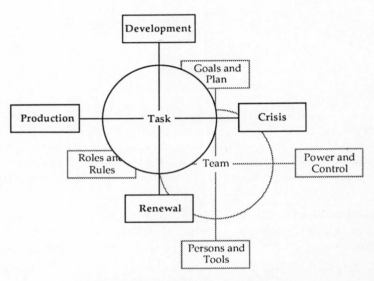

Figure 5.8 *Affinities between team tasks and team features*

There is some affinity between *production* tasks and the *roles and rules* feature of a team: the continuous and sustained production of goods or services needs a well-defined organizational structure with clear functions and job-descriptions attached to a variety of different roles, and with clear allocation of responsibilities.

There is some affinity between *crisis* tasks and the *power and control* feature of a team: dangers and emergencies require a clear and strong focus of command and command procedures in the team that copes with them. Each kind of *task* can skew the team dynamic by giving undue emphasis to the corresponding *feature* of the team: to be preoccupied with one sort of task can result in the related feature being overdeveloped at the expense of other features. I return to this point later on. Figure 5.8 lays out the affinities between different sorts of task, and different features of a team.

Motives of team members

The dynamic of the team is also strongly affected by the sources of its members' actions. There appear to be four basic kinds of motive which in various combinations can explain the behaviour of people who work in a team or an organization, and which influence the dynamic. They are shown in Figure 5.9.

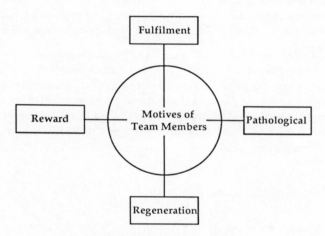

Figure 5.9 *Motives of team members*

1. Regeneration motives. Members of a team need to renew their skills and themselves: to take time to learn and develop on the job, for further education and training, including training in the use of new technology, for rest, relaxation, refreshment, recreation and inner recovery. At a deeper level, regeneration motives point to the need of people to be *self-creating:* to take charge of their own growth and unfoldment as persons. This means increasing their capacity for voluntary choice in relating to their own internal processes, and to the outer world of society and nature. At a still deeper level, they include the need for self-transfiguration: the transformation of the personality by openness to the transplanetary sphere as I described it in the previous chapter.

2. Fulfilment motives. Here we have the needs of team members to be fulfilled by what is intrinsic to the work they do. The motive is to achieve job satisfaction *per se*. People need to be *creative:* to realize, express and fulfil their human capacities, talents, values and aspirations in what they do. They need their work to be within their autonomous control; to be mentally stimulating and challenging; to engage with their special interests and abilities; to have variety and scope; to engage co-operatively with others; to be worthwhile and in a good cause, realizing some wider end.

3. Reward motives. These are the needs of team members for things that are extrinsic to the actual nature of the work itself: needs for pay, for security, for career prospects, for status and recognition, to belong to a group. These extrinsic rewards of work are part of everyone's work motivation.

4. Pathological motives. These are relatively unaware compulsions, rooted in old, repressed emotional trauma and hurt, which produce distorted, distress-driven forms of behaviour. The four classic compulsions are to be an oppressor, a victim, a rebel and a rescuer. These four pathological roles can be acted out in various ways in teamwork. The whole team dynamic can be warped by them.

The first three - regeneration, fulfilment and reward motives - are the basic triad. They can be (1) satisfied and in balance; (2) frustrated, causing much work-related distress; (3) unbalanced and overdone in some direction, because of the nature of the task, or the wider social and economic situation, or because of pressure from pathological motives. Where the team, for whatever reason, is too preoccupied with one or other of these sorts of motive, then the team dynamic and its organizational structure will be distorted.

Distorted forms of the team dynamic

Alienation or fragmentation occurs within the team dynamic, when team members become bound to one of the four main features of the team, and become estranged from the other three. The one to which they are bound develops in a distorted way, at the expense of the others. There are tendencies for certain correlations to occur between the the sort of team feature to which people become bound, the related task, and the related motive.

However, these correlations as presented below are only parts of a purely theoretical model of four types of limiting case. The dynamic of teams in the real world will be more complex and composite. The purpose of the model is to provide a template of affinities and tendencies, which may aid diagnosis within bewildering realities. It overlaps with that of Roger Harrison (Harrison, 1972; Handy, 1985), but differs extensively in the way it maps out four organizational *pathologies*, whereas he is concerned with organizational *ideologies*.

One basic principle, invoked in all the .1 points below, is that of *social inertia*: the tendency of any social form, once it has been set up in one context, to stay as it is, and to be transferred where possible without change or with minimal change to other contexts.

1. Person-bound. Teams that specialize in renewal tasks - learning and development on the job groups, staff development and training teams, recreational facility teams - tend to become person-bound, caught up in the satisfactions of self-renewal, and the fulfilment of regeneration motives. Purely personal needs and interests predominate. Decision-making power becomes subservient to the fulfilment of renewal needs: and this is at the expense of the team's social structure, and of meeting its goals and plan of work. Decision-making may tend toward the autonomous mode, each person doing their own thing. Absorption in renewal tasks can undermine all the other sorts of task.

1.1. Effect of renewal tasks on persons. When renewal tasks are sanctioned, people let their hair down, become absorbed in pursuing personal needs and interests, in reviving, refreshing and realizing themselves. Everything else tends to go by.

1.2. Effect of regeneration motives on persons. Renewal tasks, if at all imaginative and person-centred, open people up to the deeper possibilities of self-realization. Regeneration motives, once awakened and given a little scope, flower into full-blown self-actualizing motives - which can dramatically reinforce the absorbing nature of renewal tasks, and may lead a person completely to abandon their current work arena.

2. Problem-bound. Teams that are preoccupied with development tasks, as in R & D and problem-solving work, tend to become problem-bound, too absorbed in goals and plan issues, too identified with fulfilment motives. This means that decision-making control becomes subservient to a preoccupation with problem-solving tasks and the pursuit of technical know-how, and this is at the expense of a coherent social structure, and of personnel welfare. Decision-making may be entirely in an *ad hoc* co-operative mode of informal mutual consultation. Development tasks are over-emphasised.

2.1. Effect of development tasks on goals and plan. When a team is looking at new ways of doing things, its longer term objectives can get distorted by overfocus on the immediate problem: decision-making is distracted by current work from the wider sweep of goal-setting and planning.

2.2. Effect of fulfilment motives on goals and plan. Development and problem-solving tasks can yield a lot of personal fulfilment: they satisfy needs for autonomy, creativity, intellectual interest and stimulation, challenge, and so on. So the immediate absorbing intrinsic satisfactions of the work reinforce the distraction away from managing the team's longer term goals and plans.

3. Role-bound. Teams committed to production tasks, to maintaining the production of goods and services, tend to become role-bound bureaucracies. They may become more concerned with the roles and rules of their social structure than the goods and services it is supposed to produce, and too strongly influenced by reward motives. This means that decision-making power becomes subservient to the roles and rules of organizational structure, and this is at the expense of production itself, of development tasks, and of personnel welfare. Decision-making is in the hierarchical mode, perhaps after some real or nominal consultation. In a chronic bureaucracy, all four sorts of task may suffer.

3.1. Effect of production tasks on roles and rules. In order to maintain a steady flow of goods or services, the team needs a clear allocation of functions to different roles, with rules defining who does what with whom and when and how. This structure, once set up, may tend to become an end-in-itself, with those who run it rigidly preserving or enlarging its form for its own sake, regardless of changes in the product and demand in the wider world. In such bureaucratic fixation on an out-of-date form, decision-making ceases to command effective production, and is ill-adapted to crisis management, welfare tasks, and development tasks.

3.2. Effect of reward motives on roles and rules. People at work need pay, security, some status and recognition, and to belong to an organized group. A well-defined system of roles and rules can meet all these needs, offering a significant range of extrinsic rewards to the workers. Reward motives may strongly reinforce the tendency for the system to become an end-in-itself, because the more it is sustained and elaborated with status and pay scales, the more it will also satisfy reward motives.

4. Power-bound. Teams that focus a lot on crisis tasks, as in police, military and medical work, incline to be power-bound. They may tend to exaggerate power and control issues, and may be influenced by pathological motives. This means decision-making is in the hierarchical mode, without any prior consultation, in which strong central command becomes oppressive and is carried too far - at the expense of organizational structure, of fulfilling team goals, and of the needs of personnel. In task terms, crisis task attitudes distort non-critical service tasks, development tasks, and welfare and training tasks.

4.1. Effect of crisis tasks on power and control. When crises are afoot, dominant command is needed. But dominant command may also be unawarely and inappropriately transferred to non-critical service and other tasks - where its habits of mind and forms of social control are restrictive and counter-productive. The team or organization as a whole then inclines toward autocracy: it lacks the awareness and flexibility to adopt different forms of decision-making for different sorts of task.

4.2. Effect of pathological motives on power and control. When power and control are distorted into autocratic forms, under the influence of crisis tasks, they also become prey to the influence of pathological motives. The compulsion unawarely to act out repressed pain in oppressor and victim roles can readily further distort the exercise of dominant command. Those who command can become compulsively oppressive; those who obey may slip into old victim scripts. The autocracy starts to become irrational, and severely distorted.

Figure 5.10 sets out the affinities so far proposed. I stress again that reality is much more complex than these simple correlations indicate. Different motives can run into each other: thus elements of pathology may be involved with each of the other three sorts of motive. Different tasks may overlap. The model provides only initial orientation within a problem.

Distorted Form	Feature of Team	Type of Task	Sort of Motive
Person-bound	Persons and tools	Renewal	Regeneration
Problem-bound	Goals and plan	Development	Fulfilment
Role-bound	Roles and rules	Production	Reward
Power-bound	Power and control	Crisis	Pathological

Figure 5.10 *Distorted forms of the team dynamic related to feature, task and motive*

Diagrams of the distorted forms

The distorted forms of the team dynamic are shown in Figures 5.11 to 5.14. In each form, there are three levels of emphasis, represented by the size of the boxes and the size of the title in them: the most at the top and the least at the bottom, with medium emphasis in the middle. The smallest box represents the greatest casualty of the distortion.

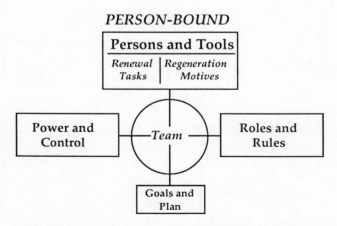

Figure 5.11 *The person-bound distorted form of the team dynamic*

In the person-bound distorted form, Figure 5.11, autonomous immersion in the satisfaction of personal learning or recreational needs is at the cost of organizational structure and clear corporate decision-making. The team can lose its way without coherent objectives and plans. A classic example is the staff development course where the members have much scope for self-determination in curriculum design. The task of planning can disintegrate in person-bound chaos and anarchy.

In the problem-bound distorted form, Figure 5.12, overemphasis on the task of innovation and problem-solving is at the expense of effective command and team structure. The challenge of a breakthrough into some new approach becomes obsessive. People become exhausted, overworked and ineffective.

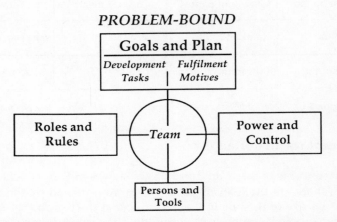

Figure 5.12 *The problem-bound distorted form of the team dynamic*

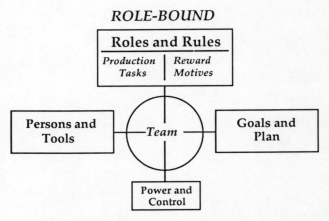

Figure 5.13 *The role-bound distorted form of the team dynamic*

In the role-bound, bureaucratic distorted form, Figure 5.13, the preoccupation with organizational structure is at the expense of the effective use of people and a rational programme that fits the task. Relevant and resourceful decision-making disappear and become totally subservient to sustaining the bureaucratic status quo.

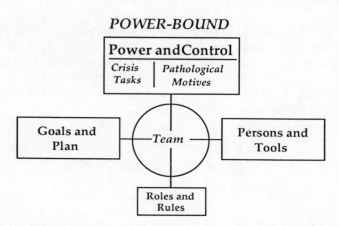

Figure 5.14 *The power-bound distorted form of the team dynamic*

In the power-bound, autocratic distorted form of the team dynamic, Figure 5.14, excessive hierarchical command and control from the top is at the expense of coherent objectives and planning, and of the effective use of people. Teams and organizations that deal with critical situations, may allow the strong hierarchical command that is appropriate at actual times of crisis, to extend inappropriately into other non-critical areas of work. There is no coherent social structure that enables this distinction to be made in practice.

Extreme forms of autocracy are caught in a vicious circle. Because of their persistent oppression, they are faced with the permanent crisis of resistance and rebellion, which reinforces the autocratic command structure.

I must stress again, that these are conceptual models only, abstract portraits of negative limiting cases. The diagnostic tool is not the patient, just as the map is not the territory. Reality is more mixed and varied. The actual team or organization may combine selective aspects from several of these models. Power-bound and role-bound forms may combine; problem-bound and person-bound forms may combine. A team at different times in its life and under the influence of different tasks may tend in each of the four directions.

There are two pairs of polar opposites. The power-bound is most at odds with the person-bound: excessive central command has no tolerance of excessive personal autonomy; and vice versa. Likewise, the role-bound is most at odds with the problem-bound: a rigid system of roles and rules has no tolerance of the unpredictable flexibility of structure involved in obsessive problem-solving; and vice versa.

The organizational context: critical issues

So far I have considered the influence on the team dynamic of the interaction between features of a team, the sort of task it has, and the motives of its members. If the team is part of a larger organization, there are also certain critical, contextual issues that radically affect the dynamic. The issues arise between the team and the organization, and this in relation to each of the four main features of the team, as shown in Figure 5.15.

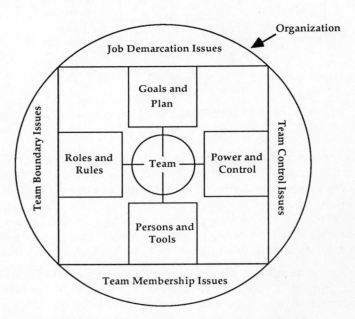

Figure 5.15 *Critical issues between the team and the organization*

1. Team membership issues. Is the right person, in terms of skills and temperament, in the right team? Does one team within the organization have a stronger claim on existing personnel than another? Can different teams share access to needed equipment and appropriate technology? The issues are to do with the persons and tools.

2. Job demarcation issues. What tasks belong to the team? Where is the line to be drawn between these tasks and those of other teams? The issues are to do with the tasks of the team, its goals and plan.

3. Team boundary issues. What marks this team off from other teams within the organization? What roles are within the team? Which ones overlap with other teams? And with respect to these, are the respective responsibilities clear? The issues are to do with roles and rules.

4. Team control issues. Does the organization control the team hierarchically, manage it consultatively, or confer upon it a high degree of autonomy? The issues are to do with power and control.

The social context: critical issues

The team within its organization, or the independent team, is set in the context of the wider society. At this interface a further range of critical issues emerge to influence the team dynamic.

Figure 5.16 shows these in a second ring around the issues to do with the organizational context.

1. Human and physical resources in society.   The range of skills and the level of skills development needed in team members raise issues about what human and physical resources there are in the wider society; about the scope and standards of education and training in the community; about the number of people with relevant skills; about the availability of equipment, goods and services, raw materials.   Such issues relate to the persons and tools feature, and to renewal tasks.

2. The rate of social and technological change.   Social structures and technology in the wider culture are changing at a rapid rate. Every team needs to adapt its tasks to these developments; its work goals and work-plan will have to be evolved into new forms.   The issues here relate to the goals and plan aspect of a team; to development tasks.

3. Staff turnover, recruitment and job description.   People change jobs, get dismissed, retire. The team has an identity and structure that is independent of any particular persons. It has to keep reaching out into the wider society to recruit people to fill its roles. The issues of staff turnover and recruitment influence job description and definition, organizational structure and career prospects - the roles and rules feature of a team.

4. Relations with other organizations.   The issues involved here have a strong bearing on the power and control aspect of a team. How are decisions made which affect the working relations between the team and some external organization? Are they made co-operatively and consultatively, by both parties having equal power?   Or are they made hierarchically, with one party having more power and influence than another?

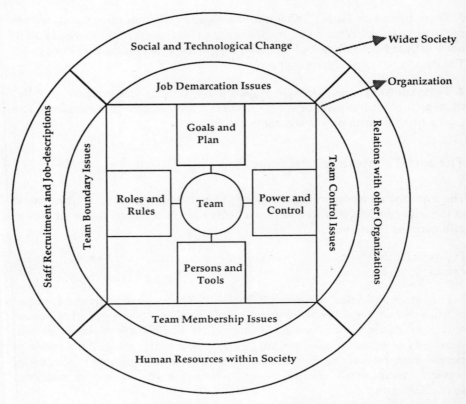

Figure 5.16 *Critical issues between the team, the organization and the wider socety*

The influence of ideology

By ideology I mean the core values of the team that define its priorities. They state what, ultimately, the team or organization is doing its task for. They define what intrinsically worthwhile state of affairs it is seeking to reliaze through its work. There seem to be four different sorts of value that can influence the team dynamic.

1. The ideology of human and planetary flourishing. The integrated value-system here is that of personal development in co-operative relations of action inquiry with others, creating self-transforming learning organizations, combining decentralization and federalism, and nurturing the eco-system of the planet. Personal development expands through the entire whole person web from the intrapersonal through the interpersonal, to the cultural (socio-structural), ecological and transplanetary spheres; and is committed to balancing self-determination, co-operation, up-hierarchy influence and down-hierarchy responsibility. See the later sections of Chapter 4.

2. The ideology of social welfare. The primary value of the team, the overriding principle of all its work, is the creation of greater welfare in the social system it serves.

3. The ideology of profit. The primary value of the team is the maximization of profit, as a result of the task, which is usually the production of goods or services of some kind. This value overflows into the value of pleasure-seeking.

4.The ideology of power. The team is dominated by those who command it, and their ideology is to value the exercise of power for its own sake, as an end-in-itself. They are interested in the satisfactions of power, and more power, as such.

These four values are not mutually exclusive. Two or more of them can co-exist in mixed proportions within the ideology of a given team or organization. They also correlate somewhat, as shown in Figure 5.17, with the affinities set out earlier in Figure 5.11.

I shall return to consider the role of these ideologies in the vision of holocracy, after the next section on the manager.

Distorted Form	Feature of Team	Type of Task	Sort of Motive	Ideology
Person-bound	Persons	Renewal	Regeneration	Human-planet flourishing
Problem-bound	Goals	Development	Fulfilment	Social welfare
Role-bound	Roles	Production	Reward	Profit
Power-bound	Power	Crisis	Pathological	Power

Figure 5.17 *Ideology correlated with distorted form, feature, task and motive*

The authority of the manager

I have so far considered five factors that influence the team dynamic: the structure of the team, its different sorts of task, the motives of its members, its social context, and its ideology. The sixth factor is the authority of the manager, which has two main aspects. Firstly, who appoints the manager; whence does his or her authority derive? And secondly, how does he or she exercise authority and control; what sort of decision-making model does he or she use? These two dimensions together create a portrait of the power of management.

Managers may be self-appointed, as with the founder of any business or other kind of organization. Or they may be appointed by those whom they then lead: I will refer to this as being peer-appointed. Or they may be appointed by some established source of authority which is over and above their own role and the team they lead: I call this being hierarchically appointed.

How managers exercise their authority in relation to the team takes us back to the modes of management discussed earlier in the chapter. They may be hierarchical and autocratic, making all decisions for the team and over it. They may be co-operative and consultative, negotiating and deciding things with the team. They may lead by delegation, giving maximum scope for autonomous decision-making within the team.

Putting these two dimensions together, we get a nine-part grid giving the basic forms of a manager's power, as shown in Figure 5.18.

Manages by ➤ Manager is ▼	Direction: hierarchical decisions	Negotiation: co-operative decisions	Delegation: autonomous decisions
Self-appointed			*Autonomy*
Peer-appointed		*Democracy*	
Hierarchically-appointed	*Oligarchy*		

Figure 5.18 *The basic forms of a manager's power*

I have entered on the grid three fundamental kinds of political system. In an oligarchy, power is conferred by a few and exercised by a few over the majority. In a democracy, power is conferred on the leaders by the people, and exercised co-operatively by means of majority vote among the people's representatives. In an autonomy, power is simply the exercise of initiative by all the individuals in it, each of whom is active in empowering an association of self-directing persons.

Leaders - self-appointed social initiators - in the political system of autonomy will be self-eliminating. Once the members of an association for self-directing people become sufficiently self-directing, the role of the initiating leader will dissolve away. Such a leaderless association will include a good deal of co-operative decision-making among its autonomous members, and for some functions the appointment of some members to rotating hierarchical roles will be appropriate. Co-counselling associations are like this.

On the smaller scale of a single team, the question is whether the terms of appointment to management specify how managers shall exercise their authority. A self-appointed manager can exercise power by any or all the modes of direction, negotiation and delegation. Democratically or hierarchically appointed managers need to make sure that they find acceptable the modes in which it is specified that they shall exercise their authority. The place or places of the manager on one or other of the three rows of the nine-part grid will have a strong influence on the team dynamic.

The vision of the manager: holocracy

I now come the final and seventh factor that influences the team dynamic - after the structure of the team, its different sorts of task, the motives of its members, its social context, its ideology, and the authority of the manager. This is the vision of the manager. The current limits of social and physical reality are a challenge to the realization of vision. And many strands now converging at the leading edge of cultural change suggest for any manager the vision of holocracy.

By this I mean that the manager - as a facilitator of personal development at the workplace - guides the team dynamic in the light of certain core values, a set of priorities organized as an up-hierarchy, in which the items listed below progressively inform, shape, support and empower those that follow later, as illustrated in Figure 5.19. The holocratic leader seeks to be a mediator, a channel, for this up-hierarchy of influence.

1. Persons and tools, and the ideology of human and planetary flourishing, are first. This means several things - at different levels.

1.1. Working hours, conditions, and facilities are such that people can maintain high standards of refreshment, renewal and recreation.

1.2. Personnel are fully educated and trained for their work. They have chosen it, are suited to it, and are fulfilled by it. They are equipped with appropriate technology, for the human relations and task side of their work, and for the eco-system of the planet. Learning in the job, for it and alongside it, extends into personal development (Mulligan, 1988).

1.3. The culture of the organization is such that it is a self-renewing learning environment, adapting and changing its form and its technology as its members, through their personal development and action inquiry on the job learn more about how to realize the holocratic vision. Thus it fulfils people's regeneration motives - deep needs to be self-creating and self-transforming. It upholds as paramount the ideology of personal development in co-operative relations with others, creating self-transforming organizations, combining decentralization and federalism, and nurturing the eco-system of the planet.

It develops technologies that serve these ends. This ideology sustains, nourishes and grounds the holocratic up-hierarchy.

Thus personal development expands through the entire whole person web from the intrapersonal through the interpersonal, to the cultural (socio-structural), ecological and transplanetary spheres; and is committed to balancing self-determination, co-operation, up-hierarchy influence and down-hierarchy responsibility.

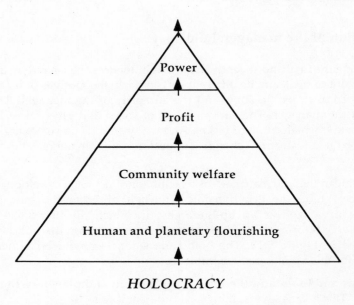

Figure 5.19 *The holocratic up-hierarchy of ideologies*

2. Goals and plan, and the ideology of social welfare, are second. The task aspect of the team, and its commitment to the welfare of the society in which it is embedded and which it serves, are subordinate to the basic ideology of 1 above - human and planetary flourishing as defined.

2.1. The work of the team makes some significant contribution to its local community - to its current welfare and to the development of this welfare into the future.

2.2. It is organized to yield job satisfaction, to gratify fulfilment motives in team members - their need to be creative, to realize their human capacities, to exercise autonomous control, to work co-operatively in a good cause, to have significant up-hierarchy influence.

2.3. The goals of the team, its work-plan and methods are under regular review, involved in and keeping pace with social and technological change in ways that contribute to community welfare; and that integrate this concern for immediate social benefit with the wider sweep of cultural, ecological and transplanetary development.

3. Roles and rules, and the ideology of profit-seeking, are third. The social structure of the team, its formal positions and job-descriptions, its allocations of function and responsibility, and the pursuit of profit, are guided first by the ideology of human-planetary flourishing and second by the ideology of local community welfare.

3.1. Roles and rules are kept flexible and adaptable, responding to the requirements of the task, the needs of persons, and the use of appropriate technology, not restricting any of these through unnecessary rigidity. The roles of owner, manager and worker become co-extensive through the increased use of worker co-operatives.

3.2. The team is structured to satisfy the external reward motives of its members - their needs for money, status, security, recognition, social belonging - in a way that is supportive of and not to the detriment of their intrinsic job satisfaction.

3.3. The pursuit of profit from the production of goods or services is enjoyed within the wider ideologies of community and planetary welfare; as, for example, with so-called ethically sound firms. Profit is not maximized through the pursuit of undifferentiated growth but set within the context of a steady-state eco-economy. There is no entitlement to profit exclusively through ownership, except through the investment of pension funds and other funds that support those who are legitimately outside the total work force.

4. Power and control, and the ideology of power, are fourth. The management of the team - how decisions are made, and the pursuit of power, are contained within and emerge from all the prior levels of the up-hierarchy.

4.1. Pathological motives are kept out of managerial action.

4.2. Charismatic authority and transforming power are used to enhance the spread of self-determination and peer supervision in the workplace.

4.3. Managers are guides who can exercise their authority in the hierarchical, co-operative and autonomous modes with equal skill, flexibly moving between them as and when appropriate in order to express this up-hierarchy of values. Crisis situations are handled with an autocracy that does not then get transferred to other non-critical areas of teamwork.

Figure 5.19 shows the holocratic up-hierarchy of ideologies as an arrow-head or pyramid. The ideology of human and planetary flourishing is the ground of the ideology of community welfare, of a social order that takes care of people; and these two ground, limit and transform the ideologies of profit and power. In terms of related correspondences, pathological and reward motives are grounded in fulfilment and regeneration motives. Renewal and development tasks provide the creative guidance and support for a self-developing culture of work on production and crisis tasks.

This, of course, is all part of a vision. The manager is seeking to mediate this vision; to engage with the tendencies within the team dynamic toward the distorted forms - power-bound, role-bound, problem-bound, person-bound - and to balance these tendencies into the holocratic form, thus facilitating personal development in the workplace.

6. Peer review audit

Autonomous meaning of work

I have suggested in Chapter 5 that the manager as facilitator of personal development in the workplace selects mode-dimension combinations to create a managerial style that progressively moves toward more delegation and employee autonomy: increased self and peer determination. And I defined the autonomous mode on the meaning dimension as delegating knowledge and data-gathering, interpretation, feedback, reflection and review to the team; so that making sense of what is going on, giving work meaning, is autonomous, entirely generated by the team. One way for the manager to promote this kind of delegation is to train people to run their own peer review audit groups. Such groups give meaning to their work by a form of self-directed quality control of job performance.

Peer review audit is a radical kind of peer supervision whereby a small group of people in the same profession or team come together in regular meetings to develop and apply standards of professional competence (Heron, 1977, 1982b; Kilty, 1978, 1980). It is quite different from peer supervision with a critical incident focus - described in the next chapter - which works with case content material and on-the-job issues, and tacitly assumes job definition and criteria of competence. Peer review audit works at a prior level: it deals directly with job definition and makes explicit criteria of competence.

The procedures are simple enough. The group defines the job and analyses it into its major component parts. It takes one such part of the job and devises a basic set of criteria for competent practice in that part. It then works out a way in which group members can use those criteria to self-assess their on-the-job competence and can keep a record of this self-assessment. Members go off and apply this self-assessment to their professional practice in the chosen part for an agreed period. Then they meet again to present their self-assessment records and to listen to, and take account of, peer feedback on them. In the light of all this they review and revise the criteria used, the self-assessment method and issues of competence in the chosen area of work. They may launch into a second cycle assessing the same part of the job. Sooner or later they will choose to move on to another part of their work, dealing with it in the same way, starting with defining it and devising criteria of competent practice of it, and so on.

What we have here is a form of professional development, a stategy of continuing education, and a method of collaborative action inquiry into professional practice. It can be used with any professional group; and I have introduced it to doctors, dentists, teachers in higher education, co-counselling teachers, managers, management trainers, group leaders, behavioural science researchers, and others.

Commitment to excellence

Every profession is faced with the big issue of how to maintain standards of competence. Keeping up to date with information and technical advances, and acquiring new skills, through ongoing education and training play an important part. But sooner or later there has to be some kind of review of what the professionals are doing and how they are doing it. Centralized generation and control of standards by means of re-examination, or by roving inspectors who sit in at the workplace, is one method. It suffers from 'big brother syndrome': centralization of this kind can lead to rigidity, dogmatism, narrowness and authoritarianism. It lacks a proper regard for individual professional flair and judgment; and by undermining these important qualities, it can lead to conformity and playing safe among the rank and file.

The other method is for the professionals themselves to review what they are up to. For in the last analysis it is personal commitment to excellence on the job that is crucial. This commitment cannot be imposed, it can only be self-generated: it is a matter of intrinsic motivation, of being fired by the deep satisfaction of doing good work. Peer review audit provides a supportive network of colleagues, and a procedural framework, within which this kind of personal motivation can flourish.

Education for the professions

There is however a major anomaly in our current methods of educating professional people. I have long argued that a fully educated person is, among other things, an awarely self-determining person, in the sense of being able to set objectives, to formulate standards of excellence for the work that realizes those objectives, to assess work done in the light of those standards, and to be able to modify the objectives, the standards or the work programme in the light of experience and action; and all this in discussion and consultation with other relevant persons. And many people, I find, agree that this sort of action competence is indeed what we can reasonably expect of an educated professional.

Unfortunately, the educational process in most of our main institutions of higher education does not prepare students to acquire this kind of self-determining ability For the staff in these institutions unilaterally decide student objectives, work programmes and assessment criteria, and unilaterally do the assessment of student work. This goes on until graduation, so that fledgling professionals are undereducated so far as the process of education is concerned: they have had no experience in setting objectives, planning a work programme, devising assessment criteria, or in self-assessment; nor have they acquired any skills in doing any of these things co-operatively with others (Heron, 1988a).

What this all means is that many professional people have emerged from an educational system which has not equipped them with the basic self-determining and co-operative competencies that are required for the effective practice of peer review audit. For this form of audit is all about setting criteria for oneself and with others, practising self and peer assessment. So training and preparation are needed, which is why I am devoting a whole chapter to the method, with considerable discussion of the facilitation issues involved at each stage.

Of course, the education system is slowly changing. A growing minority of places of higher education in some countries are introducing more student autonomy in learning (Boud, 1988). But there is still a long way to go before the majority of places use a process of learning that is truly educational.

The medical profession in the UK was caught out by the anomaly to which I have referred. In 1976 it published a high level report on Competence to Practise, in which it recommended to itself a form of audit based on self and peer assessment - peer review audit - as the most appropriate method of audit for mature professional people. It rejected any kind of audit imposed from on high by some centralized body of medical authorities, and for the same sorts of reasons which I have given above. The problem was, and still is, how to act on this given that doctors emerge from a highly authoritarian educational system, unilaterally and centrally controlled by staff. The result has been something of a developmental stalemate.

Peer review audit, then, needs a training programme, a whole workshop devoted to it. I use a two-day block followed two weeks later by another day. This gives an opportunity to go through the whole procedure slowly, taking plenty of time to look at all the relevant issues along the way. The two-week gap is for people to go off and do their self-assessments on the job; and they return to present them on the final day.

Peer assessment

There are two major issues about the whole process that I must cover before going through it in detail. Many professional people will consider it impractical to take time out during the working day to visit colleagues from the audit group and do on-the-job peer assessment of their work. So in many peer review audit groups, the peer assessment is done on the presented self-assessments, not on the actual work to which those self-assessments refer. This is still immensely fruitful as we shall see.

Where it is possible for people who do the same sort of job in the same organization and building to sit in from time to time on each other's work and do on-the-job peer assessments, this is all to the good; and I refer to this option in discussing the stages where it applies. Even so, it is still secondary to and supportive of, and does not replace, the main point and power of the method, which is self-assessment.

Practice and outcomes

The other important point is the distinction between assessing practice, what the professionals do and how they do it, and assessing outcomes, the effects of their practice on their clients, on the social system, on the natural world, on the physical artefact. Are we to look at what the doctor does, or at the effects of this on the patient? It might seem that patient outcome is the final test of medical competence. But only to a degree, since the effectiveness of many medical practices depends significantly on patient co-operation and self-help. Outcome studies may report ambiguously on both medical intervention and patient self-determination, and indeed on other unsuspected variables.

So with some other professions. There is no correlation between teachers' lecturing skill and students' examination performance, presumably because many students compensate for poor lectures by private study. Generally speaking, where the outcome of professional practice is to do with effects on other persons, there is likely to be this kind of ambiguity. Where the effect is on a physical product, as in architecture and engineering, then outcome studies are reliable: houses and bridges either stand up or collapse, and if they collapse under normal circumstances then faulty design is the cause.

Many professional groups that use peer review audit will be in one or other of the many helping professions. They will probably be wise to assess both practice and outcomes, the exact mix depending on the profession and the practicalities of gathering in assessment of outcomes in the time available. Some of the ambiguity about client outcomes can be dealt with by asking the clients themselves to report on outcomes through questionnaires and interviews. Clients can also, of course, give vital feedback on practice, since they are often at the immediate receiving end of it.

Finally, there is the possibility of peer review audit groups which include both the professionals and some of their clients. There can then be a conjoint audit of both practice and outcomes.

I now present the various stages of the audit. The first three stages are all done at the first meeting, stage 4 is on-the-job application of the audit, stages 5, 6 and 7 all occur at the second and peer review meeting, stage 8 is the second cycle of on-the-job application, and so on. Figure 6.1 gives an overview of the procedure with time allocations.

STAGES OF PEER REVIEW AUDIT	TRAINING AUDIT	SECOND CYCLE etc
Stage 1 Select area of practice Stage 2 Agree on criteria Stage 3 Devise self-assessment method	2 days maximum Half-day minimum	
Stage 4 Assessment on the job	2 weeks	4 weeks
Stage 5 PEER REVIEW Presentation: 12 minutes Questions: 3 minutes Peer assessment: 6 minutes Devil's advocate: 6 minutes Positive feedback: 5 minutes Review and plan: 3 minutes Stage 6 Review of audit procedures Stage 7 Plan second cycle If same area, refine Stage 6 If new area, Stages 1, 2, 3	1 day	1 day

Figure 6.1 *Stages of peer review audit and time allocations*

Stage 1. Select an area of practice to assess

The group members break down their professional work into its component parts, and choose one part of it, or sub-part, to audit. This is first of all an exercise in job definition, an exercise valuable in its own right. The job may need to be analysed into sub-parts or even sub-sub-parts in order to get down to an area that can be effectively assessed.

Thus a group of dentists defined their work as fourfold: clinical practice, staff management, administration, legal and financial matters. Clinical practice was further subdivided into examinations, X-rays, fillings, extractions, etc., and at this level a choice for assessment could be made.

Then the group need to select one area of practice to assess. The basic rule here is for everyone to choose the same area, so that members can pool their wisdom in defining criteria of competence for it, and get the full benefit of comparing and contrasting their performance in it. The dentists mentioned above started their first cycle with 'fillings'; another group of dentists selected 'long-term patient care over eight years'; training officers chose 'managing staff in the immediate office'; health education officers chose 'managing time on a daily basis'; doctors chose 'keeping medical records'.

Facilitation. In a training group everything depends on getting a good start, so the selection of the area of practice to assess is crucial. Here are some things to remember.

1. Job definition analysis can be done by a group brainstorm on a wall-chart, then you facilitate a group discussion which gets it into some compact final form; or by each member doing their own analysis first, then the results are compared, debated and collated. Keep the thing going into parts, sub-parts or sub-sub-parts until the group gets to assessable items.

2. Members may need some prompting about job definition areas that a narrowly conventional approach might exclude, such as emotional self-management, interpersonal skills, or ecological control. At the same time, unless there is a special eagerness to do so, the first two of these are not the obvious candidates for a first run at assessing on-the-job. Something less close to psychological base might be better for getting the feel of the method.

3. People can usually only manage to assess one area of practice at a time. Covering several areas at once is unwieldy in criteria-setting, in on-the-job assessment and in reporting back. So resist any unrealistic proposal of this kind from the group.

4. Useful guidelines for people in choosing an area are: that it is manageable for assessment; that it has a fair amount going on in it; that it excites interest and curiosity as a vehicle for assessment. There is also: its importance, that is, how much it is a key part of the job; close to this, but not the same, is whether it is symbolic of, a marker for, other areas of practice (as with 'keeping medical records' for doctors); and whether it is currently undergoing some crisis of change or stasis.

5. The job analysis and the selection of an area can run together. In other words, the group breaks the job up into certain major parts, selects one of these, then converts this into its sub-parts, and chooses one of these for the assessment. It may be too fatiguing for the group to do the whole job analysis covering all parts and sub-parts.

Stage 2. Agree criteria of competent practice for the selected area

Group members now decide on a set of basic criteria of what it is to do good work in the selected area of practice. First they have to generate some criteria, then choose which ones to use. The basic rule here is to limit the final number that will be used to an absolute maximum of six, while three or four would be quite acceptable. To have a large number of criteria to apply in on-the-job assessment in the midst of a busy professional life, or at the end of a long working day, is unrealistic. The whole format of this method has to be compact so that the motivation to use it is enjoyed and undimmed.

Dentists who wanted to assess 'fillings' used as criteria: cleared decay, retention, no ledges, supported enamel, lining, contouring. Training officers who wanted to assess their competence in 'managing staff in the immediate office' devised the following criteria: setting objectives with staff; agreeing standards with staff; agreeing time-scale with staff; balancing monitoring of staff with staff autonomy; consulting staff prior to generating policy; supporting staff.

Facilitation. Because mainstream higher education still does not educate and train people to generate criteria for their own work, this stage needs a lot of attention, with trainees being given much support on various issues. People often seem to enter a sudden mental fog when asked to generate criteria of competence for what they do. The culture has conditioned them to be punitively judged, and the distress about all this clouds the mind for a while, until they start to get a feel for what it is to be creatively and happily self-assessing. Here are some of the main issues to consider.

1. I usually recommend that group members first write out individual lists of criteria for the chosen area of practice. This gets them in the way of thinking about criteria. Then these lists can be presented all together on a wall-chart for everyone to see and discuss. Then the thing can go any one of three ways. People can stick with their own individual criteria; or they can collate and edit these until they all agree on a consensus list so that everyone is using the same; or they can agree that each person can use any three or four from the total unedited pooled list, so they may use some of their own and some of other members. The more technical the practice with physical outcomes as in dentistry, architecture, engineering, the more important it is to have consensus criteria; the more socially interactive the practice, the stronger the case for the mixed model, the third way, which seeks to balance the claims of idiosyncratic personal values with the claims of the collective wisdom of the group. This issue can be debated within the group. As usual it is best to support whichever way seems to motivate people the most. It can always be modified in a later cycle of the audit.

2. Criteria occupy a simple kind of logical structure which is hierarchical. Ask a dentist what good clinical practice is and he will say good examinations, good X-rays, good fillings, good extractions, etc. Ask what a good filling is and he will say good retention, good contouring, etc. Ask what good retention is...and so it goes on. A good outcome is defined by a sub-set of outcomes, and each good sub-set item is defined by a further sub-sub-set of outcomes, etc. Similarly, a good practice is defined by a sub-set of good practices, and each good sub-set item is defined by a further sub-sub-set of practices, etc. And the hierarchy can go on endlessly into the minutiae of good outcomes or good practice.

Group members need to grasp this basic structure and accept that for the purposes of doing an effective audit, they need to come to a resting place quite soon in the hierarchy and just assume as tacit the criteria for doing well the sub-practices or sub-outcomes they have chosen as criteria for doing well the main area of practice or outcome they want to assess. Thus the dentists assessing fillings, using as criteria the outcomes of cleared decay, retention, no ledges, supported enamel, lining, contouring, intuiting the more detailed evidence for each of these things being in good order. What is interesting about all this is that the assessment ultimately rests on an *intuitive feel for a good pattern* in the practices or outcomes used as criteria.

3. There are practice criteria and outcomes criteria: the former are about what the professionals do and how they do it; the latter are about the effects of their practice on their clients, on the social system, on the natural world, on the physical artefact. I discussed this important distinction in an earlier section, where I suggested that it is probably wise to audit both practice and outcomes where possible. The dental group that wanted to assess their work on fillings used only outcomes criteria to do with the end-result in the mouth of the patient, such as cleared decay, proper retention, etc. But they could and perhaps should have used equally important practice criteria to do with the sequence of working, the tools to use, etc.

Outcomes criteria are related in a special way, *other variables notwithstanding*, to standard good practice criteria. If the practice is good, the outcomes are good. But this relation is asymmetrical. For it does not follow that if the outcomes are good then the standard good practice criteria must have been applied. The same good outcomes, or even better ones, may be the result of some total innovation in practice that departs radically from the standard. However if the outcomes are bad, then we can conclude that at any rate the standard good practice was not followed. So if only outcomes criteria are used, we either know, with negative outcomes, that standard good practice was not used, or we do not know, with positive outcomes, whether standard practice or innovative practice was used. Try to use both outcomes and practice criteria.

4. Where the outcomes criteria are defined by professionals in terms of the reactions of other people, then it makes sense at some point for the professionals to ask those people whether they agree that such responses are for them a sign of good practice. Such agreement is a meta-outcome criterion: it is a higher order outcome criterion for choosing first-order outcome crtieria.

Stage 3. Devise a self-assessment method for practice on-the-job

I call this a self-assessment schedule. It is both a method for assessing myself in the selected area of practice, on-the-job, according to the chosen criteria; and it is a way of recording this self-assessment so that I have some clear data to bring to the next peer review meeting. If the area of practice is one that has a lot of different instances, like a dentist doing fillings, then the method needs to include some form of sampling the practice, otherwise continual assessment will overwhelm the job. It is also valuable, wherever possible, to buttress the self-assessments with assessments from relevant others.

The dentists assessing fillings did the assessment over 20 working days before the next peer review meeting. Each day they self-assessed two fillings immediately after completing them. These fillings were chosen 'at random' by the dental nurse, but only after they were done. Each dentist had a sheet with horizontal rows for the two fillings for each of the 20 days, and the six criteria (cleared decay, retention, no ledges, supported enamel, lining, contouring) in vertical columns. For each filling they entered a rating between 1 and 5 under each criterion: 3 was a minimal acceptable standard, 5 was excellent and 1 was 'lousy'. After the ratings there was a space for notes on any special features of the filling or comments that would help the dentist remember it. This sheet was the basis for presenting their self-assessments at the peer review meeting.

The training officers assessing their competence in 'managing staff in the immediate office' kept a daily diary of staff management activities with sufficient detail to key in their memory to the events that occurred. Variations they proposed were: record only pertinent activities, record everything and underline pertinent activities, record both what you do and what you do not do. At the end of each daily entry in the diary they scored themselves, for each of the criteria they had chosen out of the pooled group list, on a rating scale from 1 to 5: 1 was very low competence, 3 was medium competence, 5 was very high competence. Each rating had an explanatory note attached saying why it was pitched where it was. An optional extra, depending on personal preference and local circumstance, was to ask one or more of the staff being managed to assess the training officer, using the same criteria and rating scale, over the whole period of the on-the-job assessment. All this data was brought to the next peer review meeting.

After this stage members disperse to do their on-the-job assessments, so at the end of this stage they need to decide over what period they will do these before the follow-up review meeting. And if any members of the group are going to be available for each other as peer on-the-job assessors, then the planning of this needs to be agreed.

Facilitation. There are several design issues in devising an effective and workable self-assessment schedule for use on the job. It is as well to have a good grasp of them when assisting a training group to work through this stage.

1. While self-assessment is primary and cannot be replaced by assessments from others, the latter are powerful adjuncts to the former: so encourage people where possible to use on-the-job assessments of their work by peers, by other staff and by clients. On-the-job assessment by peers means that a professional equal, ideally one of the peer review audit group, is present during the relevant work and assesses it on the spot, using the agreed criteria and rating scale. Other staff doing different kinds of work in the same team can give vital assessments under certain criteria; and so of course can clients, who are perhaps the most under-used, primary source of feedback for all professionals. Other staff and clients can also be consulted about the criteria they are being asked to use and may well want to propose modifications that represent their perspectives more fully.

2. If the professionals do a lot of the sort of work they want to assess, then they have to assess samples of it. Too much sampling and assessing is a distraction from working, so the whole audit becomes self-defeating; but too little and the audit loses validity. So the potentially conflicting claims of the work and the audit have to be reconciled. In the early stages it is better if the claims of the work have precedence over those of the audit. Too much rigour, time and energy going into the audit, and people will rapidly lose motivation to sustain it. It is better for a group to devise a modest schedule of sampling and assessing, so that it has a good chance of being applied in a continuous way. As well as the frequency of sampling being modest, the recording and scoring needs to be simple and accessible.

3. Who chooses the sample? If you choose it after the event, you can bias your sampling by choosing only the best instances. If you choose it before the event, you can boost the event by making sure you perform well. This seems best: to choose the sample before doing the work brings out the virtue of running a self-assessment schedule, which is that of itself it promotes good practice. Those interested in some more 'random' selection can do something like the dentists, who asked the dental nurse to choose the work to be assessed after it had been completed. But even here the virtue still works, since if any piece of relevant work may be called to account and you do not know which, you will be that bit more diligent with each of them.

4. The assessment can be done immediately after the work has been done, or later in the same day on the basis of memory. It all depends what sort of work it is. Leaving assessment until the day after or longer is hazardous, unless there are good audio or video tapes, or comprehensive descriptive notes or recorded data. One approach is to keep good descriptive notes of relevant instances in a daily diary, then assess a whole batch of such instances after a few days, dealing with each one in turn.

5. The use of a rating scale for each of the chosen criteria is really a way of marshalling an intuitive feel for a good or bad pattern in the instance of it. Or, to put it another way, it is an intuitive way of applying the next but tacit and unformulated sub-set of criteria. It is important to stress again that, however elegant the self-assessment schedule and the analysis of the criteria, in the last anaylsis the whole thing comes down to an *intuitive feel for a good pattern* at the workface of practice and outcome.

Stage 4. Assessment of practice on the job

Group members now disperse back to work to apply the self-assessment schedules on the job for an agreed period before meeting again for the peer review. Dentists assessing fillings chose 20 working days, training officers looking at managing staff in the immediate office opted for 7 working days. In a training audit this period will usually be decided in advance by the facilitator and the institution organizing the event.

Facilitation. The main issue is how long this period of on-the-job self-assessment is to last. If it is too short, there is no time for the virtuous effect on practice to build up momentum, and no adequate sample of behaviour is taken. If it is too long, then commitment to sustain the audit may falter through lack of peer support and stimulus. Less than a week seems too short, and more than four weeks seems too long at any rate for an early stage of audit.

Stage 5. Peer review: self-assessment presentations

This is in many ways the most critical part of the whole procedure. The whole group meets and each member takes it in turns to share with the others his or her on-the-job self-assessments and any additional assessments from peers, other staff or clients. Each presenter gets feedback from the other group members, being confronted on avoided weaknesses, and on underplayed or omitted strengths: interpersonal skill is needed here. The presenter then reviews his or her overall self-assessment in the light of this feedback; this may lead over into a personal action-plan to take account of the findings.

A group of teachers in higher education, in a peer audit training programme, used the following format for each person in their peer review. This is a standard format but clearly there can be many variations of it. The teachers were working in sub-groups of five or so.

Stage 1. Presentation (12 minutes). The presenter describes the activity being audited, the criteria used, the self-assessment method and frequency and method of sampling used, how thoroughly or forgetfully the auditing was done; and then shares an overview of his or her on-the-job self-assessments, and assessments by peers, other staff and clients, using charts, scores, notes, anecdotal material to demonstrate and support stated strengths and weaknesses. He or she may also identify relevant enhancing or distorting circumstances; and close with some general estimate of his or her current level of competence with respect to the area of practice under audit. This is done from a designated place in front of the group. The peers give sustained, warm, empathic and uncompromising attention, without comment at this stage.

Stage 2. Clarifying questions (3 minutes). The peers then ask any questions which help them understand more fully what has been said, which clear up obscure parts of the presentation, or which open up important and relevant but unstated information. There is no feedback at this stage.

Stage 3. Peer assessment (6 minutes). Any peers present who made on-the-job assessment of the presenter's work, using the same self-assessment schedule, now give details of it, also using charts, scores, notes, anecdotal material to demonstrate and support stated strengths and weakenesses. If it was not possible for the presenter to get on-the-job peer assessment of this sort, then this stage is omitted. If this stage is included, it is still followed by stage 4.

Stage 4. Devil's advocate (6 minutes). Where there is no peer assessment stage this is the central part of the peer review, so far as peer feedback is concerned. The ground-rule here is that the peers can amplify the least doubt, unease or uncertainty, as well as put forward obvious doubt, unease or uncertainty, about the presentation. The title 'devil's advocate' gives permission for this amplification, which gives this stage its effectiveness. It is a subtle assessment of the self-assessment presentation, and can be extremely telling in what it picks up. It is a stage in its own right and is not just there to compensate for the absence of any on-the-job peer assessment. What the peers are listening for here and amplifying in their feedback are: what has been overplayed, underplayed, and omitted, and this in relation to both strengths and weaknesses. So the peers need to remember and tune in for these six categories: overstated strength, understated strength, omitted strength, overstated weakness, understated weakness, omitted weakness. The evidence for them will be either obvious or lurking in either the manner or the content of the presentation. And the manner is just as important a source of evidence as the content.

The presenter listens to all this without any comment or reply, dissociating from any temptation to get into defensive, self-justifying reply. His or her task is to use great discrimination, discarding what is misconception or projection, taking on board what is telling and perceptive, even if uncomfortable; and in this way mentally refining his or her original self-assessment.

Stage 5. Positive feedback (5 minutes). Here the peers give their unqualified appreciation and affirmation of what they valued about the presenter, the manner of presentation, the format of the presentation, and the quality of the work being reported on.

Stage 6. Presenter's review and action plan (3 minutes). This time is optional. Some presenters will simply want to digest the whole experience and will not yet be ready to express any review or devise an action plan. Others may want to take this time to revise their self-assessment in the light of the feedback, and to make some action plan about how they want to modify their future practice in the area that has been assessed.

Facilitation. There is a host of issues in the above set of six stages, and I shall only mention some of the major ones.

1. The above sequence takes either 29 or 35 minutes, depending on whether there is any peer on-the-job assessment available. So with a group of five, we are talking here of two and a half to three hours of extremely intense and concentrated work. Groups have shown a remarkable commitment to sustain this, because of the rewards and challenges involved. But there needs to be a time-keeper for each presenter; and the time-keeper will also facilitate the pacing, reminding the presenter of how much time is left during any stage, and prompting the person to keep to basic data and not get overwhelmed by detail. If there are eight people in the group, it will be essential to have a break of 20 minutes or so after four of them have taken a turn.

2. It is usually relevant for the presenter to say something about his or her thoroughness in doing the self-assessment. It is good to encourage people to have a ground-rule of being entirely open and honest about this; and to encourage people to take their turn no matter how loose or forgetful their auditing was. It is easy enough for the clamour of work and consequent fatigue to drown out the claims of self-audit, and people need support and affirmation through this stage.

3. Remind both presenters and peers to keep an eye on the six categories: overstated strength, understated strength, omitted strength, overstated weakness, understated weakness, omitted weakness. Remind peers to keep an eye out for them not only in the content of the presentation (what the person says about work incidents, about the criteria and using them, about the self-assessment method and data), but in its manner, that is, the selection and use of language, the tone of voice, facial expression, posture and gesture, the emotional undertow of what is being said, hints of unfinished business from the person's past, etc. And remind presenters that our competitive and emotionally repressive culture conditions us through insecurity both to make false claims about our performance, and to be self-deprecating about our real strengths.

4. Both in the peer assessment round and in the devil's advocate round (stages 3 and 4) it is essential for people to learn to give feedback in a manner that is not punitively judgmental, that is free of malice or hurtful attack, and that is fundamentally respectful and supportive of the person to whom it is addressed. This is a basic interpersonal skill: to avoid mollycoddling and evasion on the one hand, destructive sledgehammering on the other, and find that high ground between them that combines love with a statement of the unequivocal and the uncompromising. The facilitator with a training audit group can interrupt every distorted bit of feedback and invite its author to rephrase it until he or she gets it clean and feels what it is like to say it clean. Given clean feedback, it is important for the devil's advocate round to become rigorous and exacting, for the feedback to include references to manner as well as content of presentation, and to confront the presenter as much with intimations of understated and omitted strengths as about anything else.

5. When people give positive feedback in stage 5, it is useful if they can keep a balance between appreciating particularities to do with the work reported on, the manner of presentation, the format of the presentation, and the qualities of the whole person.

6. While this peer review sequence is a central and dramatic part of the whole audit procedure, it is the training facilitator's task to remind people that it is designed to affirm the primacy of self-assessment while making the fullest use of the discriminating assessment of others. The purpose of peer feedback is not to cow the presenter into conformist submission, but to provide a powerful crucible in which he or she can refine his or her self-assessment, and to enhance personal commitment to excellence.

Stage 6. Review of audit procedures

As a lead-in to this review, it is a good idea if everyone in turn gives a more detailed account of their use of the audit procedures, especially during the on-the-job audit. This was covered briefly at the opening of the self-presentations, but now is the time to go into it more thoroughly. This is a self-assessment now of one's past self-assessment competence on the job. How often did you remember, or forget, to do whatever your schedule required? If you forgot, did you try to catch up by doing self-assessments in a batch rather than one by one at the time as you should have? How thorough was your recording and scoring? How honest was it? What difficulties were found in applying the criteria, and in using the schedule? Did motivation and commitment stay the course or not? Did you notice any good or bad effects on daily practice of using the procedures? Do you want to keep on doing this?

On the basis of these disclosures, group members now review all the relevant procedures. These are: the criteria used; the method and frequency of sampling; the method of self-assessment; the method of assessment from others; the method of record-keeping; the amount of time spent on the job between meetings; the self-presentation procedure at the follow-up meeting. They may propose changes to some of these or not as they judge fit.

It is valuable for the group to do this review before members decide whether to continue to audit the same area of practice as before, or whether to change over to look at another part of their work. This is the decision the group makes next.

Facilitation. This stage is a meta-audit of the basic audit and is important to do before continuing any further with the basic audit.

1. Group members need an opportunity to share openly not only their successes and failures in using the method, but also what they make of it in terms of interest and usefulness, and whether indeed they want to go on with it. This is done in the opening part of stage 6. This is the personal experience part of the meta-audit.

2. In reviewing all the methods used, the group moves on to the procedural part of the meta-audit. Sometimes people have difficulty shifting from assessing their work to assessing how they have been assessing their professional work, and keep slipping back from the latter to the former. Then the facilitator needs to keep re-routing them.

3. In revising the methods, the members are effectively making them their own. Too many modifications rapidly introduced will probably mean a degeneration: people will be avoiding the challenge and discipline of the original model, whose rationale they have not fully grasped. I have not yet encountered this: on the contrary, participants seem to be invigorated by the rigour of the model and are anxious to preserve its basic format.

Stage 7. Planning the second cycle

Group members now decide whether to continue to audit the same area of practice chosen for the first cycle or whether to select some new area. If they proceed with the same area, then they will only need to refine the revisions already made in stage 6 to the criteria, the method of sampling and frequency of sampling, the method of self-assessment, the method of assessment from others, the method of record-keeping, the amount of time spent on the job before the next review meeting.

If they opt for some new area of practice to assess, then they go through stages 1 to 3 again, no doubt a lot quicker than the first time, since people will by now be familiar with the logical geography, and some of the self-assessment methods devised for the first area will transfer over to this second area of practice.

At this stage, the training officers assessing their competence in 'managing staff in the immediate office' decided to continue auditing the same activity but homing in on aspects of it which the self-assessment presentations had highlighted as needing more attention. This meant they refined and focussed more sharply their account of the activity and modified the original criteria accordingly. They kept to the same on-the-job self-assessment schedules.

Facilitation. We are now coming up against issues of time management, so I will mention this issue first.

1. Stages 5, 6 and 7 are all being done at the same meeting. Stage 5, if done in a presentation group of not more than five people, takes from two and a half to three hours, effectively a whole morning. Stages 6 and 7 can take an hour each, so we are talking a whole day or two half-day sessions here. I will return to issues of time management further on.

2. The more basic issue in stage 7 is to do with convergence and divergence. If the group continues to converge on the same area of practice cycle after cycle, it masters that area thoroughly, but at the expense of integration with mastery of other areas. If on the other hand the group diverges at each cycle from one different area to another, the mastery of all areas is integrated, but minimally since each area is minimally mastered. Every group has to solve this equation according to its own situation and preferences. One solution is to add a new area of practice at each cycle, while continuing on a skeletal audit from the previous cycle, so with every cycle you are doing a major and a minor audit. Another is to do two cycles for each area, and every few cycles do a global audit (see below). It is all a matter of ingenuity and enterprise to work out a suitable formula.

Stage 8. The second cycle of on-the-job self-assessment

The group is now busy on the job, auditing either the same area of practice as on the first cycle, or a different area. An indefinite number of cycles is now under way, involving some formula for balancing convergence and divergence, mastery of parts with mastery of the whole.

Facilitation. The single main issue here is for how long a peer group runs an audit, before taking a break to lie fallow and let the effects of the prior audit phase work as an unstructured creative yeast. Each group will decide this on their own account, according to local variables. But the principle seems clear that peer review audit needs to be run in phases with significant non-audit periods in between.

Peer review audit and the experiential learning cycle

It is instructive to construe the audit cycle in terms of the primary and secondary experiential learning cycles discussed in Chapter 3. The secondary cycle starts with stages 1, 2 and 3 of the audit in the conceptual mode, analysing the job, devising criteria and a self-assessment schedule. It includes stage 4 which goes into the practical mode, working on the job.

Stage 4 in turn contains the on-the-job self-assessments which constitute a series of primary cycles. These include the practical mode of the job, at the heart of which is the audit in the affective and imaginal modes, involving the feel for a good pattern at the workface, and the conceptual mode for the self-assessment scoring, and so back to work in the practical mode.

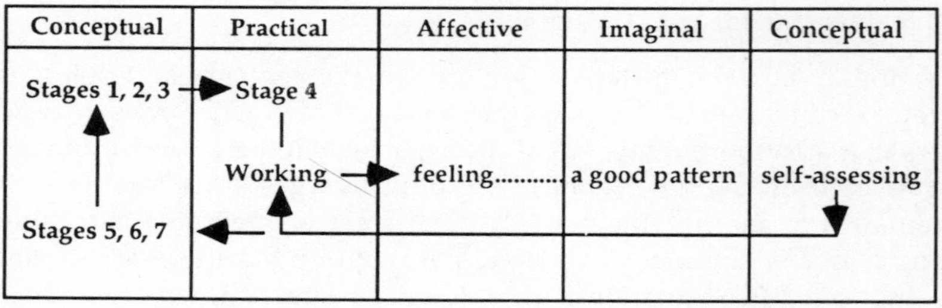

Conceptual	Practical	Affective	Imaginal	Conceptual
Stages 1, 2, 3 ➤	Stage 4			
	Working ➤	feeling..........	a good pattern	self-assessing
Stages 5, 6, 7				

Figure 6.2 *Peer review audit and the experiential learning cycle*

The primary cycles continue throughout stage 4, until there is a return to the secondary cycle in the conceptual mode with stages 5, 6 and 7. Figure 6.2 illustrates the sequence, and brings out the sophisticated nature of peer review audit as a form of action inquiry and action learning. The bedrock of the whole process is the feeling for a good pattern of practice and/or outcomes.

Further issues

1. Training. For reasons stated in the opening section of this chapter, people need initiating into peer review audit through a training programme. I use a two-day block for stages 1, 2 and 3, with a two-week gap for stage 4, on-the-job audit, followed by a one-day session for stages 5, 6 and 7. Once trainees start on stage 8, the second cycle, they are on their own, although they can always call in their original trainer as a consultant for occasional sessions.

2. Time management. To get an audit started, it needs a minimum of a half-day session, to take people through stages 1, 2 and 3. I have launched audit programmes with a half-day session, but on a full training programme I prefer an opening two-day block so as to have plenty of time to create the right climate, to take each of the first three stages slowly and consider all the issues, and to do other back-up exercises. Once an audit gets going, it needs a whole day or two half-day sessions between cycles of on-the-job self-assessment. Half a day is for the presentation of self-assessments, the other half for reviewing the methods used and preparing for the next cycle. If each cycle is four weeks, then peer review audit means a day a month. See Figure 6.1.

3. Time discipline. Every stage and part of a stage needs a clear time allocation and the group needs to be disciplined in keeping to its time boundaries. The job of time-keeper can be rotated round the group. The time-keeper can also be responsible for pacing things, for moving the group along so that it covers all the relevant ground in the time allocated.

4. Process discipline. The group needs to monitor its use of feedback, especially during the devil's advocate round in stage 4, and make sure that it is clean. The role of process guardian can be rotated round the group if people feel the need for it.

5. Size of the group. Two people can do an effective peer review audit, although of course they are short on peer variety and peer feedback. Eight is probably a maximum number, especially for the presentation of self-assessments. With 20 or so people on a training programme, I usually work in groups of five.

6. Composition of the group. The basic premise is that the group consists of peers from the same profession. But there are important variations. You can have a hierarchical group within the same profession; for example, a group of hospital doctors that includes a consultant, senior registrar, registrar and junior house doctor; or among teachers, the head, the deputy head, a head of department, a senior teacher and a junior teacher.

Another radical variation is to have mixed practitioner-client audit groups. The professionals audit what they do, and their clients audit what they do in response to what the professionals do. But they work together through all the stages, contributing to each other's different content. There there can thus be a very effective conjoint audit of both practice and outcomes.

7. Comparable audit groups. Several peer review audit groups within the same profession can run concurrently, and for a time independently. Then they can meet in inter-group exercises to compare and contrast: job definitions, practices identified and chosen for audit, criteria used, central issues of practice to emerge, and so on. In this way a profession can explore its own developing culture: the constancies and variations in values, norms and practices. The intergroup session can also compare the various audit methods used: sampling methods, self-assessment schedules, the use of assessment from others, record-keeping, time on the job between meetings, self-assessment presentation procedures, stages of the audit, and so on.

8. Co-operative inquiry. Peer review audit as it stands is a form of peer group action inquiry in the sense in which I have used this term in previous chapters. As such it can readily be included within the format of a full-blown co-operative inquiry - into professional standards, competence, culture and practice. Co-operative inquiry does research with people, not on them: the researcher co-opts the subjects as co-researchers, and joins the subjects as co-subject. In short, all those involved are both co-researchers in devising, reflectively managing and drawing conclusions from the research, and also co-subjects in experiencing and doing whatever it is that the research is about. They cycle several times between reflection as researchers and action as subjects, and use a variety of validity procedures to keep themselves clear of consensus collusion and other hazards of the method.

I and others have written about this kind of non-alienating research at length elsewhere, advancing central arguments for it and reporting examples of it (Heron, 1981a,b; Reason and Rowan, 1981; Reason and Heron, 1986; Reason, 1989). Peer review audit is a collaborative action inquiry which cycles between reflection at group meetings and action on the job: it is already ripe for inclusion in the co-operative inquiry format.

9. Process commendation. The point of peer review audit is lost if the standards generated and confirmed by one group for itself are used to dictate professional behaviour to any other group or the profession at large. The process is more important than any prescriptive products, and it is this process which is to be commended to other groups within the profession, so that they can generate their own dynamic standards.

10. Global audit. I have stressed the importance for beginners of not taking on more than one area of practice, so that they are not over-taxed in getting to grips with the basics of the method. But once they have done so over a few cycles, then they can consider the possibility of the occasional global audit, which I mentioned in stage 7 above as a way of balancing the claims of convergence and divergence. A global audit takes the whole job as the area of practice, and treats each of its main parts as criteria of competence. It then uses the principle of intuitive feel for a good pattern in scoring performance under each criterion on, say, a five-point scale. This audit uses very broad brush-strokes in keeping diary notes of performance, and in self-assessment of that performance. It is too imprecise for the beginner, but can be very fruitful after someone has mastered the more precise format by looking at a small part of the job.

7. Peer support groups

This chapter continues the theme of facilitator authority being used to enhance the emergence of self and peer determination in independent groups that, once launched, run indefinitely without any dominant facilitator. Such groups combine holistic learning with autonomy in the learning process, allied with co-operative support from peers. 'Peer support group' is a generic term for any kind of group in which people meet on a regular basis to help each other develop their personal or professional lives in the world. It is peer run, with an agreed structure within which members may rotate time-keeping and other roles, and has no permanent leader. The structure can be reviewed at intervals and revised in the light of consensus experience. I have discussed one special kind of peer support group - peer review audit - and there are many more of less rigorous format which can have a liberating and transformative influence. In this chapter I review just a few of these.

In our emotionally repressive, competitive society, in which competence anxiety abounds amid mutual fear and suspicion, people need encouragement and guidelines to start peer support groups. Hence the case for including the experience of an appropriate kind of group towards the end of a training programme. The facilitator can propose an initial format, have people try it out, then gather in feedback afterwards and in this context raise consciousness about the various issues involved in running it effectively.

The argument for peer support groups runs as follows. 1. Persons are only persons in active relation with other persons. 2. Persons develop holistically in autonomous learning relations with other developing persons in reference to real-life situations. 3. A culture or sub-culture ceases to be oppressive, and starts to be enhancing only when its members meet in small groups to revise its norms, values and social practices in their individual and collective lives, personal and professional. 4. A liberating culture is one which is self-generating and self-renewing through autonomous, whole person, peer learning and inquiry.

All this follows from the thesis of Chapter 4 that persons are to be defined in terms of their intentional involvement in personal, social and planetary transformation: intrapersonal change is realized in interpersonal change, which is manifest in cultural change, thence in ecological and transplanetary change. This is the up-hierarchy influence. Peer support groups provide one sort of immediate arena in which this whole process can be launched. The groups provide a focus for experiential learning in living. In terms of the primary and secondary experiential learning cycles discussed in Chapter 3, the primary cycle is learning through living intentionally in the world, the secondary cycle includes both the primary and the review of it at the group sessions.

Peer support groups can deal with personal life, professional issues, or the interface between the two. When they deal with professional issues, I call them peer supervision groups: these will usually have members from the same profession, to get the benefit of insider know-how. But there is also a case for the occasional mixed profession group, where, in effect, other members will give an intelligent lay person's view of what the focal member presents. I have known experienced doctors benefit greatly from lay feedback on situations of deep professional concern.

The agenda of peer support groups can cover difficulties, problems and thorny issues; or affirm joys, successes and creative achievements. It may uncover what is past, examine what is current or prepare for the future. It is invariably committed to transformation, either in the sense of enhancing the value that is present, or manifesting the value that is absent. And it may use imaginal techniques, analytic techniques, emotional techniques or practical techniques.

Running a peer support group

1. Meetings can be for 2 to 3 hours every 2 to 3 weeks.

2. With a membership pool of 15 people, an average of 8 or more may attend at each session. Not everyone will want a turn at each meeting.

3. Those who want a turn say how much time they each need and negotiate until the turns fit the total time available. Turns may be of different lengths. In some types of group, every turn may be of a fixed length.

4. The person who takes a turn says how he or she wants to divide the time and to use each portion, and asks another member to keep time and call out when each portion is up. It works best if people keep to the discipline of their overall time, although they may want to rearrange the size of the portions once they get going.

5. The group may want to allow time for a short opening and closing ritual, and, before the closing ritual, a few minutes for a brief process review of how the session has been for everyone, including any ideas for procedural consciousness-raising. And after ten sessions or so, the group will need a whole session for an extended review of the method, of its strengths and weaknesses, possibly leading to major or minor revisions of the format.

Helpful ground-rules for a peer support group

1. Be co-operative, supportive, and non-competitive.

2. Find strength in the acceptance and disclosure of your growing points, where you are vulnerable, unknowing and unskilled. Avoid any kind of window-dressing and image-building in what you present.

3. Listen fully to others and attend to what they say and how they say it and how they are being and what they are doing when they say it.

4. Give both positive and negative feedback with an equal sense of the worth of the person to whom either is addressed.

5. When giving negative feedback, make sure it tells the truth with love, and is free of either evasive pussyfooting, or punitive sledgehammering.

6. Give the group a committed priority in organizing your time; and attend the group whether you need to take time in it for yourself or not.

I now give a selection of peer support group methods which I believe are particularly valuable, starting with those that have a professional focus - which I call peer supervision - moving on to the professional/personal interface, and ending with those that are concerned with personal life. There is nothing especially sacrosanct about the various formats, and while they have been tried and tested, new groups may well want to introduce creative variations to suit their own needs and interests. For a summary account of a wide range of methods that peer support groups could incorporate see Huczynski (1983).

Peer supervision: critical incident focus

Members bid for time, and each one who takes a turn divides it into three portions. The whole procedure is given in summary form in Figure 7.1.

Stage 1. You lay bare some critical issue from recent or current professional practice, something that exposes you to your limitations, that presents a challenge.

Stage 2. You hear a statement from each of your peers, listening carefully and without entering into any dialogue with them, except to ask the occasional clarifying question. Suppose you have described some recent problematic encounter with a client, then your peers can comment in any one or more of the following ten ways:

1. They may raise an issue about what the client has said or done, or not said or not done; and in general about the client's state and situation.

2. They may focus on your interventions in relation to the client.

3. They may attend to the relationship and the process between you and the client, including all aspects of transference and counter-transference.

4. They may deal with wider contextual issues to do with the organizational and cultural patterns of oppression within which you and the client are set.

5. They may comment on how you have presented the problem, the story-line, the choice of language, the tone of voice, the nonverbal manner, and draw some inference from this about what you are carrying from the encounter, or what you are mirroring about the encounter with the client, or about the wider context.

6. They may disclose their own images, phantasies, thoughts, feelings, of a kind that seem to have been irrationally stirred up by what you are saying, and present this as their reception of something unaware going on in you and in your relation with your client or with the wider context.

7. They may share their own experience of a similar kind so that you may learn something from it by way of comparison and contrast.

8. They may offer some relevant piece of information, or refer you to some useful article, report or book, or suggest you talk to a colleague or friend of theirs.

9. They may offer policies or practical strategies for you to consider using on yourself, your client or the process between you and your client, or in relation to the context.

10. They may invite you to do some piece of personal work on yourself, or some skills practice through role play, here and now in front of the group.

STAGE 1	STAGE 2	STAGE 3
	Your peers take it in turn to comment on any one or more of the following:	You choose to do one or more of the following:
You present a critical incident/issue	The other Your intervention The relationship The wider context Your presentation Their inner reactions Similar experiences Relevant information Practical strategies Invitation to work	Review opening presentation Make an action plan Personal development work Projected rehearsal

Figure 7.1 *Peer supervision: critical incident focus*

Stage 3. You can do one or more of the following three things.

1. You can review your opening presentation in the light of what your peers have said, and note which of their comments you need to take on board, after

discriminating selectively amongst them. It is important that this does not degenerate into a defensive rejection of those you do not want to accept.

2. You can make an action plan, in which you commit yourself to try out certain behaviours in future incidents of the sort you have been presenting.

3. You can engage in some piece of personal development work pertinent to the issue, either self-directed or facilitated by a member whose competence you respect.

4. You can practise some relevant skill through the use of a short role play, trying out interventions that you were unable to make and that would be useful in the sort of situation you reported. This is sometimes called projected rehearsal.

Facilitation. Here are some useful tips for the facilitator to remember when introducing and monitoring the process as part of a training programme.

1. It is helpful if group members are familiar with the ten different sorts of statements they can make, given above. Each member needs to get more and more skilled in using the whole repertoire; and the members as a team need to balance the various sorts when giving feedback to the one who is taking a turn. In this way the feedback will be multi-perspectival, giving an in-depth reflection of what has been presented. Peter Hawkins and Robin Shohet (1989) have written a comprehensive book on supervision which is full of fruitful ideas which peer supervision groups can use.

2. Comment and feedback of any sort is contaminated and offensive when it includes words such as 'ought', 'should' and 'must'. Suggesting practical strategies, no. 8 on the list, needs to be free of any kind of patronage.

3. A key issue throughout the whole procedure is how much the presenter is (a) caught up in rigidities and compulsions that are run by unresolved distress from the past, (b) held up by limiting conventional assumptions derived from a rigid social system, and (c) the victim of simple ignorance and lack of skill, or (d) involved in some combination of these. Peer feedback that can help raise consciousness supportively about these matters is useful.

4. When people take their turn as presenter, they need to give some thought to the length of each of the three stages, and to have some idea of what might be best for the final stage. A piece of personal work or the rehearsal of a skill at the end may need more time than a selective taking on board of what the peers have said. Over several turns, there is a tendency to avoid these two action methods by always choosing the verbal summing up. The group needs to have a clear contract and commitment about the relevance and importance of the action methods.

5. It is a good idea for people to be flexible about how they divide their overall time. On different occasions they may want to allocate very different proportions to the three stages. They may also want to rearrange the stages, for example, presenting a problem first, then doing some personal work or a skills building role play, then gathering in feedback from their peers.

6. Members may want to record their peers' comments on audiotape, or to ask someone to act as scribe and write down what they say.

7. Diana Cortazzi and Susan Roote developed a model of illuminative incident analysis for a group of staff who work together as a team. The team members choose a critical incident in which they have all been involved, each person represents this with a drawing, then takes it in turn to exaggerate the drawing in order to probe the attitudes and actions of those involved (Cortazzi and Roote, 1975).

Peer supervision: good news analysis

In this group, members bid for time and divide their time into three parts.

Stage 1. You present some piece of your own professional practice that went well: you describe what happened first, and then seek to identify what factors contributed to your success. There are four sorts of factor here: what is going on in your client; in you the practitoner; in your client-practitioner interaction; in the wider social contexts of which either or both of you are part.

Stage 2. The peers can now give: supportive feedback on the manner of presentation; supportive feedback in terms of subliminal impacts, images, thoughts, sensations, energy movements, that occurred in them during the presentation; their affirmation of and agreement with the presenter's account of contributing factors; their opinion about what other factors may also have contributed to the presenter's success.

Stage 3. You say anything else you need to say after the peers have spoken, and you again affirm and celebrate what you have done and what you have shared.

Facilitation. The idea of this group is to get learning, motivation and uplift out of good news. When introducing this experience within a training programme, the facilitator needs to alert people to several issues.

1. It is important that the exercise is entirely free of subtle competitive window-dressing and image-building, with members tacitly vying with each other to parade their successes. So it is as well to encourage them to enjoy the celebration of genuine competence in a spirit of mutual support, and to eschew the displacement of insecurity into aggressive accounts of real competence or bolstered reports of pseudo-competence.

2. One way a group can control for this is to have a fallback devil's advocate procedure. If members feel that the manner of a presentation is aggressive-competitive or its content is phoney, they put on a special hat such as a sombrero, kept ready in the wings. This announces that they are about to speak as the devil's advocate. They then give their confronting feedback. Anyone else who supports the feedback, takes the hat and says so. Anyone who disagrees says so, in this case without the hat. The presenter does not respond to any of this, but listens attentively, taking on board what he or she needs to hear, and continues the presentation modifying it or not as he or she thinks appropriate in the light of the feedback.

3. Some members may be uncertain and diffident about their successes, or feel they have to be able to report a big piece of good news, a real triumph of skill or caring or creativity. A good ground-rule here is that effective micro-events are as important to share as valuable macro-events.

Good news analysis complements critical incident focus (covered in the previous section), so sessions of the latter can be interspersed with some sessions of the former, or vice versa; or a group could experiment with alternating between the two. What is clearly important is that peer supervision groups do not fall foul of the idea that all learning and development comes from processing mistakes and confusions. The affirmation and analysis of success is extremely potent in generating further growth.

Peer supervision: actual practice

This is a good model for counsellors and psychotherapists, although demanding. It has four main stages.

Stage 1. The group members agree on a basic set of criteria for assessing the competent practice of one-to-one psychotherapy and write these up on a wall-chart. A set of six criteria works best, because it is manageable for feedback rounds (see below). The set may include things like: not falling foul of counter-transference; giving space for client self-direction; commanding a suitable range of interventions; and so on. Reaching agreement on this set may take up the whole of the first meeting.

Stage 2. At the next meeting, one of the group starts the thing off by saying he or she wants to be the first client. This means being a real client, with something real to work on. As in the market place this client chooses any one of the other members to be their therapist. It is a ground-rule of the group that when chosen for this role you do not demur.

Stage 3. The therapist member works with the client member for 30 minutes. It is best to have a standard time for this which applies to everyone taking a turn as therapist. This means that all therapists and clients have parity of opportunity. Half an hour gives both of them enough time to make some useful headway, while giving space for perhaps two other 30 minute sessions at the same meeting.

Stage 4. Immediately after the session, the therapist gives him or herself feedback in the light of the agreed criteria, then the client gives the therapist feedback in the light of the criteria, and then everyone else in the group does so. In each case the person giving this feedback looks at both strengths and weaknesses under each criterion. The therapist may want to take notes of all this, or appoint a scribe to do so, or record it on audiotape. The therapist just listens to the feedback and does not respond or comment, but can ask clarifying questions. He or she may simply want to digest it, or may want to revise his or her original self-assessment and say which bits of feedback he or she is particularly aware of needing to take on board.

This whole process is then repeated perhaps another two times in the same meeting, with each self-appointed client choosing a different therapist from among the group. Sometimes just two sessions in a meeting will be quite enough for the time and energy available.

As well as a brief process review at the end of each meeting, there will be the periodic whole meeting process review, at which the format and the set of criteria are reappraised and perhaps modified.

Facilitation. This kind of peer supervision is rigorous and exacting. It generates considerable anxiety among members until the group is under way and gets used to the exposure. Here are some of the main issues that can arise.

1. The therapist's self-assessment can sometimes degenerate into blaming the client for being a bad client. There needs to be a ground-rule that the client or other group member will interrupt this when the therapist, or anyone else in their feedback, slips into it. While it is impossible for no reference at all to be made to what the client was saying and doing, in general the full focus of the feedback needs to be about the therapist's performance. In one group of this kind I was in, the first therapist to take a turn got into blaming the client through sheer anxiety.

2. The complementary degeneration to that of hunting down the client is for group members to scapegoat the bad therapist and attack someone in an overdetermined way for evident incompetence. What is needed here is supportive and uncompromising consciousness-raising about the weakness, not displacement of group members' distress into destructive punishment.

3. There is a further degeneration of tacit consensus collusion to the effect that 'I will be gentle with your performance so that you will be gentle with mine'. Feedback praises good points under each criterion and plays down or ignores the bad points. The meeting becomes anodyne with an excess of mutual approval. This needs to be exposed and interrupted.

4. The short process review at the end of each meeting can be used to check to what extent, if any, these three degenerations occurred during any of the feedback sessions.

5. This form of peer supervision is, in effect, a sort of short-term peer review audit (discussed in detail in the previous chapter) which combines self-assessment with immediate peer assessment on work done. But the work done is a one-off on someone in the group, whereas a real peer audit group of therapists would be assessing work done over a period of some weeks with regular clients. So I think this is best classified as a radical form of peer supervision.

Peer supervision: veridical report

This model was developed by a group of medical practitioners which I initiated into peer supervision in West London and proved to have great staying power. Its virtue, and the learning derived from it, depend on its simplicity and the integrity of the participants. I will describe it in medical terms, but it can be applied by other professions.

One basic clinical entity, such as hypertension, or low back pain, or middle ear disease, is stated in advance as the topic. At the meeting you take turns to state exactly and truthfully what you actually do in such a case. The ground-rule here is that you are ruthlessly honest and report veridically what you practise in the privacy of your consulting room. This is a warts and all account: it includes intuitive or improper shortcuts, obsessive over-caution, deviations from or elaborations of standard procedure, innovations and eccentricities and alternatives, as well as conventional routines.

Other members can ask clarifying questions about what you have reported, but they do not pronounce judgment on it or give an opinion about it. Both in the reporting and the questioning it is a foul to use the words 'should', 'ought' or 'must'. And the word 'foul' is called out by anyone or everyone if any of these words are used.

What is going on in such a group is that as the different and absolutely veridical reports are presented side by side, each member is making comparisons and contrasts among all of them, and especially with his or her own. What this leads to, for each person, is a significant tacit reappraisal of standards of competent practice in relation to the clinical entity being reported on. But each person comes away with an idiosyncratic set of revised standards. Of course, standards are not always revised; existing ones may simply be confirmed.

Facilitation. The effectiveness of this group as a form of peer supervision entirely depends on the fullness of the veridical reports. When I attended a process review of the medical group that had been using this model for some time, it became clear how members had soon discovered that if the reports degenerate into window-dressing and false image-building, the whole thing loses impact, becoming soporific and pointless. It was their high standard of honesty that had given the group its long life.

Peer supervision: projected rehearsal

This is a good model for people who are embarking on a phase of innovation in their professional practice, such as teachers in higher education who want to introduce holistic learning or more student self-direction into their classes, or traditional verbal therapists who want to start using client-centred action methods. What they need is an opportunity to overcome the anxiety of trying out something new and to build up confidence and finesse in doing it. This is where projected rehearsal comes in: practising the actual professional behaviour in a role play with one's peers (Maier et al, 1975).

It is also a good model for those who are introducing change at the political level, that is, proposing innovation at committee and board meetings or individually to senior (or junior) staff.

Once this group is under way, each meeting will open with report-back time for accounts of what has been carried through from previous role plays into real-life action. This is followed by the main part of the meeting, which is practice time for rehearsal in new role plays. After bidding for practice time, each protagonist in turn goes through the following procedure.

Stage 1. Divide your time into three parts: the first is for your proposal and feedback on it; the second is for your role play and feedback on it; the third is for final review and reflection, and a practical commitment. The second period is the main one and needs to be the longest. Appoint a time-keeper to move you on from part to part.

Stage 2. You outline what you wish to practise, with whom you will apply it in your work and your reasons for wanting to do all this. Then sketch out a provisional role play design.

Stage 3. Your peers give you feedback and comment on these intentions. They may endorse what you have said, or build on your design. They may explore the reasons you have given, or the wider contractual and contextual issues. They may raise issues of appropriateness on behalf of the recipients of what you intend. They may suggest revisions of what you wish to practise or of the role play design.

Stage 4. You digest all this, take it on board or not as you are moved, make a final statement about your role play design and what you are going to do in it; then coach group members to play the roles of the real-life recipients.

Stage 5. Do the role play and if you feel at all dissatisfied with any part of your performance, immediately halt the play and keep re-running that bit, with feedback from your peers on each re-run, until you and your peers are happy with it. Your peers too can halt the play, propose feedback and a re-run as soon as they see you throw away your power and slip verbally or posturally into anxiety, insecurity and defensiveness.

Stage 6. Your time-keeper now moves you on to the final stage of review, reflection and commitment. Review the whole practice and reflect aloud upon it, then hear your peers do the same, and let this lead into a group discussion of the central issues.

Stage 7. Make a closing commitment to follow through on this practice in real-life in a specific situation on a stated date; and to report back on how it went at the next meeting after that date.

The next meeting opens with report-back time in which each person who has something to report takes a minute or two to do so and to listen to whatever the peers are moved to say. Sometimes members may want to replace their practice time with an extended report-back time because they got in a tangle when trying something out on the job and need to get clear about it, in which case they can use the critical incident format given above. Another model is to alternate a projected rehearsal meeting with a whole meeting of report-back - using the critical incident format - on real-life application.

Facilitation. When running a projected rehearsal session in a training programme, there are some key points for the facilitator to underline.

1. The main learning is in the practice, especially the re-runs based on perceptive feedback. Encourage people to learn the art of multiple re-runs, often on quite small areas of behaviour - a phrase or a sentence and its associated vocal and nonverbal manner - in which personal power is lost and thrown away. The protagonist keeps the re-runs going and modifies them until he or she feels what it is like for that bit of behaviour to carry power rather then lose it. Also exhort people to learn to notice those verbal and nonverbal cues - in themselves and in others - in which the loss of power is evident, so that they can give effective feedback.

2. It is always best if protagonists give feedback to themselves first, so they get used to self-observation and self-assessment and do not become dependent on the perceptions of others for their self-knowledge. Even when you, as facilitator or peer, interrupt role plays because protagonists have given away power in a phrase, you still ask them first what they notice about what they have just said and done, before you give your perception of it.

3. The important thing is to make sure the biggest block of time is devoted to the actual performance of the role play, and to move people on promptly from stage one of talking about it, to stage two of doing it. Newcomers especially will put off the challenge of learning through action by discussing the issues involved, the background factors and everything else that delays the moment of experiential reckoning. This changes once people have come to terms with the risks involved and are exhilarated by the outcomes.

4. What is usually at stake when someone is contemplating introducing innovation in the classroom or anywhere else is their projected anxiety about being rejected by the recipients. Once their behaviour when introducing the innovation is in the grip of this anxiety, then it makes the anxiety self-fulfilling: the behaviour is so off key and disempowered that it produces rejection. The chapter on charismatic training deals with this issue in depth and many of the methods described there need to be applied in projected rehearsal. Basically, people need to learn in action to put their personal power forth in a manner that elicits excitement and positive anticipation in recipients.

Peer supervision: confession dinner

This is another classic medical model, which I have developed for any profession.

Stage 1. The group members meet for a meal.

Stage 2. When it is over and the group is entirely alone without possibility of interruption, a bell is rung and there is silence.

Stage 3. Anyone who is moved to do so rises to their feet and makes confession of just one item, which may be anything from among the following sorts of misbegotten behaviour.

1. Gross professional negligence or error, whether from ignorance, inadequate skill, carelessness, laziness, self-interest, irresponsible delegation, fatigue, illness, irrational compulsion, drunkenness, addiction or any other inadequacy. This covers neglecting to do something vitally important for the client's welfare; or doing something entirely mistaken; and in both cases with unpleasant consequences for the client. There is clearly a gradient here: in the medical case it runs from the unnecessary removal of the patient's appendix to the unnecessary loss of the patient's life. And each profession will have its range from the minor to the major disaster.

2. Gross professional misconduct: while the previous item is about negligence or error within the occupational task, this one is about stepping right outside the bounds of the role into abuse of the client. There is verbal abuse, denigrating, criticizing, swearing and yelling at the client; physical abuse, hitting and kicking the client or causing other grievous bodily harm; sexual abuse, from seduction through harassment to rape; mental abuse through false information, false doctrine, rejection, threat, exploitation of transference, malicious hypnosis or suggestion, overcontrol and domination; financial abuse through devious extraction of money, gifts and property.

3. Gross unsolicited behaviour: here the professional is within the occupational role, but doing major things to or for the client without the client's consent, approval or even their knowledge. This is a basic infringement of the client's right to self-determination and to be consulted about every important action being taken on their behalf.

Stage 4. After the statement, the bell is rung three times followed by a short silence while everyone takes in what has been said. Then there is a round of applause, which is intended to affirm the person who has spoken for owning and bearing witness to their malfeasance.

The same person may declare any number of items, but each is dealt with separately, followed by the bell, silence and applause, before the next one is announced.

There is no discussion about or comment on any confession that is made by anyone, either at the meeting or afterwards at any time: everyone takes an oath to this effect at the opening meeting. The only exception to this is at a periodic process review meeting when the whole procedure is reviewed and perhaps modified. One issue that may arise at such a meeting is whether what people are confessing to is appropriate and falls within the guidelines given above or within whatever other guidelines the group has given itself. Particular confessions may well have to be mentioned as evidence in making one's point in such a discussion. Also at issue may be how members are making their confession, and again instances may need to be cited.

The purpose of having a dinner first is to create an ambience of solidarity and mutual support, but any other group activity that has this effect could equally be used.

Facilitation. The main issues in setting this up or recommending it are to make sure people follow the central ground-rules: there are no eavesdroppers of any kind when the confessions start; there is no comment at any time by anyone about any confession; each confession, even from the same person, is followed by the bell, the silence and the applause; members stand to make their statements. The group can appoint one of their number to be the manager of all this throughout the session, and to interrupt any infringements.

Peer supervision: the personal/professional interface

This is a group in which professionals can explore the interaction between their personal and professional lives, issues at the interface. One format to use is the 'critical incident focus' described above. Another is to adapt 'healing the memories' below, and work on the wounded child within the professional helper: perhaps the most radical and far-reaching approach.

Peer support: life-style enhancement

I now move on to consider peer support groups that focus on personal development issues in the widest sense, although it is important to stress that such issues can include all work-related matters. This first one on life-style enhancement is perhaps the most broad-ranging.

Stage 1. At its first meeting, the group generates a wall-chart that covers all the main life-style areas. It may want to pin this up in the meeting room as a general backdrop to its procedure. A life-style map will cover something like the following main categories, although every autonomous group will come up with its own and different version.

1. *Socio-economic.* Place and type of residence; money and finance; occupation and career planning; social roles/class; cultural minority status; nationality.

2. *Interpersonal.* Friendship, acquaintanceship, colleagueship; intimacy, nurturance, sexuality; gender; parenting; cohabitation; family of origin.

3. *Basic self-care.* Social support networks; body care, health and hygiene; pleasure, fun and recreation; culture of the imagination; coping with emotional and physical trauma.

4. *Extended development.* Continuing education and training (personal development, interpersonal skills, technical skills, professional competence, hobbies/interests, academic study); creativity and expression; social and political action; ecological and planetary concern; psychic and spiritual unfoldment.

Some groups may prefer to do without a life-style map, since any map makes each item look too cut off from everything else, whereas in reality all aspects of a life-style interact.

Stage 2. At the next meeting the group will start with those who want it bidding for time. When presenting, you divide your time into three parts, and in the first part choose any area of life that you want to enhance by developing or changing it. You describe your situation saying what is going on, how active or inactive you are in the area, how satisfied or dissatisfied, how liberated or oppressed, and whether you want to leave it as it is, modify it or change it dramatically, and in what way you want to modify or change it. The area can be chosen because there is some problem or deficiency in it; or because it appears to be entirely placid and contented. In other words, you can start with difficult terrain or challenge easy ground. You may also want to adventure into new territory and talk about entering some life-style area that you have never gone into before.

Stage 3. The next part of your time is for peer feedback to which you listen without comment except for asking the occasional clarifying question when you do not understand properly what is being said. Your peers can comment on many things about your account: your attitudes and actions in the area; the other people involved; the processes going on between you and them; the circumstantial factors; the wider social and cultural context; your positive and negative assessment of the situation; your account of wanting to change it or not; what is implicit in the manner of your presentation; what subliminal impacts, images, feelings and energies they were receiving during your presentation; their own related kind of experience; any relevant information; a pertinent strategy for you to consider; a proposal for some action method for you to use in your final part.

Stage 4. The final and third part of your time as presenter is to have a final review of the issues in the light of what has been said, or to make an action plan, or to do some personal development work that is evoked by the presentation, or to use a role play to practise some behaviour pertinent to changes you want to make. The last two of these may need more time than the first two, so it is well to have a sense, when dividing your time at the beginning, of how you want to use the last part of it. You can also combine two or more of these if there is enough time.

Facilitation. This three-stage procedure mirrors that of critical incident focus in peer supervision for professionals, as in Figure 7.1, but with some additional items the peers may comment on. The same sorts of useful tip are relevant for the facilitator to remember when introducing life-style enhancement as part of a training programme.

1. It is helpful if group members are familiar with the many different sorts of statements they can make when giving feedback. They are listed above in the account of stage 3. Each member needs to acquire skill in using the whole repertoire; and the members as a team need to balance the various sorts when giving feedback to the one who is taking a turn. In this way the feedback will be multi-perspectival, giving an in-depth reflection of what has been presented.

2. Comment and feedback of any sort is contaminated and offensive when it includes words such as 'ought', 'should' and 'must'.

3. A key issue throughout the whole procedure is how much the presenter is (a) caught up in rigidities and compulsions that are run by unresolved distress from the past, (b) held up by the oppressive conventional assumptions of a rigid social system, and (c) the victim of simple ignorance and lack of skill, or (d) involved in some combination of these. Peer feedback that can help raise consciousness supportively about these matters is useful.

4. When people take their turn as presenter, they need to give some thought to the length of each of the three stages, and to have some idea of what might be best for the final stage. A piece of personal work or the rehearsal of a skill at the end may need more time than a selective taking on board of what the peers have said. Over several turns, there is a tendency to avoid these two action methods by always choosing the verbal summing up. The group needs to have a clear contract and commitment about the relevance and importance of the action methods.

5. It is a good idea for people to be flexible about how they divide their overall time. On different occasions they may want to allocate very different proportions to the three stages. They may also want to rearrange the stages, for example, presenting a life-style issue first, then doing some personal work or a skills building role play, then gathering in feedback from their peers.

6. Members may want to record their peers' comments on audiotape, or to ask someone to act as scribe and write down what they say.

Peer support: celebration, affirmation and visualization

The purpose of this group is to build on strengths and accentuate the positive. Everyone takes equal time. There is no bidding for time, or some people 'not needing' time. The commitment is that you always take a turn, especially when you don't feel like it. Each person's turn proceeds in three stages which are paced over the time available.

Stage 1. You celebrate, without negative qualification of any sort, what is going well for you currently in your life, or what recent event was good news, or what remoter past event was good news. You may mention several events, but you keep to one basic theme, so the events are all instances of the same theme. Everyone applauds.

Stage 2. You frame the same theme into a strong verbal affirmation, a positive direction for your life now and in the future, and repeat the affirmation slowly, aloud, several times, varying the language until you get it feeling right. Everyone applauds.

Stage 3. You visualize and describe out loud very precisely and clearly a future event in your life which thoroughly fulfils this theme. Everyone in the group says together 'This will be so'.

Facilitation. When taking people through this for their first time, remind them that life is full of large and small jewels, buds or seed-pods of experience that often seem to get left by the wayside, their potential unfulfilled, their promise prematurely abandoned or swept aside in the pressure of the day. Remind them also that every day has hints of what it could be, if the fullness of personhood within were creatively manifest.

1. Interrupt, and train group members to interrupt with a friendly but clear signal, any drift into negative qualification in stage 1. In the same way make sure that the affirmations and the visualization, stages 2 and 3 respectively, are free of any such qualification. This means the presenter keeps revising the same statement until it is free of both verbal and nonverbal detractors.

2. Some members may be diffident about good news in their lives, or feel they must report a big piece of good news. A good ground-rule here is that very small positive happenings and choices are as important to affirm as the large ones; or even more important because of their hidden potential. So too with long-past events.

3. Occasionally by the principle of opposities, strong unqualified celebrations and affirmations may flip the presenter into distressed memories from his or her personal past. It is definitely not the purpose of the method to induce this kind of flip, nevertheless it can sometimes occur. If this is a minor flip with not much charge on it, it is best to ignore it and just refocus the mind on the positive statements. If it is a major flip, with the presenter already in catharsis, then it makes sense to go with it and clear it.

Co-counselling training, or the equivalent, can be useful here (see under 'healing the memories' below). After clearing it, then the presenter gets right back on track with the celebration, affirmation or visualization. Those in the group with appropriate skills can rotate the role of cathartic facilitator, whose job it is to take the presenter through the release until it is appropriately cleared for that time.

4. In order to keep the exercise free of insecure posturing and deluded self-inflation, the group can be trained to use a devil's advocate procedure. If members feel that the manner of a presentation is posturing or deluded, they put on a special hat such as a sombrero, kept ready in the wings. This announces that they are about to speak as the devil's advocate. They then give their confronting feedback. Anyone else who supports the feedback, takes the hat and says so. Anyone who disagrees says so, in this case without the hat. The presenter does not respond to any of this, but listens attentively, taking on board what he or she needs to hear, and continues the presentation modifying it or not as he or she thinks appropriate in the light of the feedback. This method has to be handled with great skill. It degenerates badly when it is used by someone in the group who is too distressed to acknowledge a genuine celebration.

Peer support: projected rehearsal

This is the same procedure as that given above under 'Peer supervision: projected rehearsal'. Here it is used to practise behaviour for some impending event in one's personal life that is felt to be challenging, threatening, demanding, or whatever. It can be used by both women and men to practice being assertive in future situations where they are likely to lose personal power or give it away.

Peer support: healing the memories

This is a group in which people support each other in healing the wounded child within. In an emotionally repressive society, the wounded child within each adult is a universal phenomenon, and an increasing number of practitioner-theorists acknowledge this point (Miller, 1987). Many people go to a psychotherapist to deal with this, but one of the problems of professionalizing the process of healing - with resultant imbalance of roles and power - is that the therapy situation can only too readily reproduce the original abuse all over again.

Another approach has been the use of peer self-help psychotherapy groups. The one that I have most experience of, and can vouch for, is co-counselling as practised by groups affiliated to Co-counselling International (Heron, 1979). This is the method I would recommend for a peer support group working with the wounded child. Those who want to use it will need to go to a basic co-counselling training, which is available in most main centres.

Co-counsellors work in pairs, taking it in turns to be client and counsellor. Thus in a two-hour session, for the first hour A is client and B is counsellor, and for the second hour they reverse roles. Co-counsellors are trained in a range of simple strategies which undo the repressive barrier holding down memories of childhood trauma and distress, and provide for the reliving of the memories and the discharge of the distress. So there occurs the catharsis of grief through crying and sobbing, fear through shaking and trembling, anger through harmlessly directed storming sounds and movements, embarrassment through laughter. The point of this release is the spontaneous insight which follows it, leading to a re-evaluation of the hurtful childhood situation that caused the distress, and a reappraisal of one's current life free of projected hidden trauma. This combination of old pain released and restructuring insight gives a person more inner freedom to live their life less driven by the compulsions of the wounded child within.

The techniques are used by the client in a self-directed way as much as by the counsellor on the client. And this strong affirmation of the possibility and practice of client self-direction, saves co-counselling from some of the abuse problems of traditional one-way therapy, where techniques tend always to be in the hands of the therapist.

A peer support group using this method can break up into co-counselling pairs for a series of shorter or longer sessions, with changes of partners for each session. Sessions can be on whatever each client wants and needs to work on; or in some sessions the clients in every pair can work on the same theme. Another powerful option is for the group to stay as a whole and each person in turn takes an equal amount of time to work on what they want, or on an agreed theme. Each client can choose to work in an entirely self-directed way, or with just one other chosen person as counsellor. In either case, the rest of the group give intense, sustained supportive and silent attention.

Facilitation. The major facilitation issues affecting a group of this sort will have been dealt with at the basic co-counselling training. They relate to the techniques used, the roles of client and counsellor, different contracts between client and counsellor, the importance of equal time, never more than one counsellor when clients take turns in a group, the quality of attention in the counsellor, the balance of attention in the client, and so on. The peer support group can rotate at each meeting the role of facilitator whose sole job is to co-ordinate group decision-making about how to structure the total time available.

Peer support: invoking the empowering future

Healing the wounded child redeems the past; its complement is a form of peer support which invokes the empowering future. It is helpful if members of this group happen to have done some co-counselling training or are otherwise competent in regression work; but it is not at all essential, for this group looks entirely to the future. Members can either work in pairs taking equal turns to be invoker and witness, or can take equal turns as invoker in the whole group with everyone else being witnesses.

What invokers do is to assume a strong psychic and spiritual affinity with quite specific creatively advanced and worthwhile future events, and the people involved in them. These events are well beyond the likely span of the invokers' earthly lives. So they choose a time well into the future, say 300 years hence, when things will be very different from now, but not so different that the imaging power falters with doubt and uncertainty. They tune in and feel this time ahead, and then start to allow the images that form, whether visual, auditory or kinaestheic, to become more and more distinct by describing them fully. What they are describing is a real situation with real people in a real environment in a real part of time and space on this planet: it just happens to be in the future.

Towards the end of their time, the invokers describe how their current lives can be empowered by drawing into them, and shaping them with, some of the liberating and creative aspects of the future scenes they have envisioned.

Facilitation. What this exercise needs is that people have faith in their ability to feel the future and in their imaging power. So it is as well for the facilitator introducing this method in a training session to affirm clearly both these competencies in everyone present.

1. Encourage invokers to go with their imagery, however slight and faint, and to describe it immediately. The description fosters the imagery, and the imagery empowers the description. Once this mutual enhancement takes off, remarkably clear scenes will come before the mind's eye or ear or kinaesthetic sense.

2. Occasionally by the principle of opposites, envisioning a positive future may flip the invoker into distressed memories from his or her personal past. It is definitely not the purpose of the method to induce this kind of flip, nevertheless it can sometimes occur. If this is a minor flip with not much charge on it, it is best to ignore it and just refocus the mind on the future. If it is a major flip, with the invoker already in catharsis, then it makes sense to go with it and clear it. This is where co-counselling training can be useful. After clearing it, then the invoker gets right back on track and is off into the future again.

3. The witness gives abundant supportive attention to the invoker, and makes no comment on and asks no questions about what the invoker describes as long as the invoker is going well. But when the invoker falters, seems to lose faith in the images and slows down the description, then the witness can ask questions that help to develop the flow of imagery and descriptions. Otherwise the witness only bears witness.

8. Structural change

Personal development and structural change

The peer supervision and peer support groups so far considered will tend to have as their outcome minor or major transformations of individual behaviour, in the sense of people developing existing values in their lives or realizing new values. These individual transformations can start to have some effect in changing the face-to-face quality of life in the surrounding culture. As I said at the outset of the previous chapter, a culture ceases to be oppressive, and starts to be enhancing when its members meet in small groups to revise its norms, values and social practices in their individual lives, personal and professional.

In terms of my model of the person as a web of relations - intrapersonal, interpersonal, cultural, ecological and transplanetary - the cultural impact of the groups I have discussed is mainly as a result of work done in the intrapersonal and interpersonal domains. What I want to look at in this chapter is personal development and action inquiry construed as cultural transformation that works directly at the cultural level, addressing cultural issues as such.

By my culture I mean my mother tongue, and the social structures - the associations and organizations - within which my life is conducted, with their established roles, practices and rituals, their pervasive values, norms and beliefs. If I emigrate from the culture into which I was born, then I have two cultures, the one I bring with me as part of my history and the one I have moved into. To sharpen the discussion I shall use the terms 'social structure' or simply 'structure' and 'structural' to cover all that I mean by culture.

Three kinds of structural theory

To be committed to structural change presupposes some theory about what is wrong with current structures and about an alternative way of ordering society. On the diagnostic side, there are three sorts of theories that I believe are relevant and need each other, but are often found in total divorce from each other.

The first kind is to do with psychosocial dynamics, which depicts the interlocking of personal pathology and social pathology. The second is about political-economic macro-analysis, identifying corruptions of political and economic power in light of moral values and notions of a just social order. The third is to do with the transpersonal and is about social structures in relation to spiritual reality and the life divine.

An example of the first sort of theory about psychosocial dynamics is given by Jackins (1983) who holds that the repressed, wounded child within is stuck in a rigid pattern which includes a maladaptive victim response plus an internalization of the oppressive behaviour that caused it: the pattern has recorded in it the external oppressor's behaviour. He extends this theory of the distress pattern to generate a theory of social oppression. Persons who carry such a pattern will act out the internalized oppression against themselves as self-invalidation, and against people in their own oppressed group or in other oppressed groups within society. This effect of the oppressed oppressing the oppressed through the internalization of old external oppression, is its most damaging effect.

Certain oppressions play a key role in society in relation to other oppressions. Jackins singles out the oppression of young people by adults as the foundation for the installation of all other patterns of oppression. So far so good, but thereafter the theory rapidly degenerates into a millennial form of neo-Marxism, extremely vague on structural reform and totally devoid of any transpersonal awareness.

Theories about political-economic macro-analysis have a distinguished history from Plato's *Republic* through the views of More, Rousseau, Fourier, Godwin, Owen, Blanc, Proudhon, Bakunin, Kropotkin, Marx and many others. A contemporary example of this tradition, refreshingly free of doctrinal bias, is provided by the Movement for a New Society which sprang out of a Quaker action group formed in the late 1960s and based in Philadelphia (Gowan et al, 1979).

They criticize the society of the USA as based on the private profit system whereby people can accumulate wealth through passive ownership thereby resulting in a massive concentration of economic, political and military power among a small elite - at the expense of real democracy, distributive justice, the planetary eco-system and the third world. However, their powerful analysis is not related in any way to psychological pathology in the individual, nor to the transpersonal dimension of human experience.

An example of an extreme transpersonal account of human culture is provided by Wilber (1983) who regards both individual persons and the cultures they generate as illusory substitutes for absolute spirit: they are projections of a hidden and denied longing for spirit, projections which displace this longing in a false and misbegotten direction. The end result of this kind of theory is that the only really valid moral imperative is for people to practise meditation so that they can lift themselves out of the illusions of personhood and cultural pursuits and enter 'non-dual awareness'. This theory reduces psychosocial dynamics and political-economic processes to nothing but spiritual pathology, and leaves everybody looking for the nearest guru to effect their transcendental release.

Wilber's view is an extreme form of transcendental reductionism: it fails to honour the divine as One and Many, reducing the Many to illusion and acknowledging only the One. What is needed, by contrast, is a vision of personhood and culture as potential expressions of divine manifestation and differentiation within the realm of the Many. Self-transfiguring persons in self-transforming cultures become a creative enterprise with living divinity.

Liberation within and from the human condition

It seems to me that these three kinds of theory need each other, suitably adapted and amended to engage with each other. The idea that the oppressed need to work, psychologically, on the internalized oppressor and interrupt its tendency to oppress other oppressed people, replacing this with mutual aid, needs balancing with clear ideas about structural reform and how progressively to realize it. But this combination of the psychosocial approach and the political-economic structural approach is concerned, quite properly, with liberation *within* the human condition. To be effective I think it needs to be complemented by liberation *from* the human condition. As I have said, I do not mean by this a rejection of the human condition as illusory, but a transformation of it by knowing it as included within the subtle realms and the life divine. On this view the human person is an expression of divine multiplicity, unfolding through transfiguration into ever greater differentiation and manifestation.

Opposition actions and fulfilment actions

The words 'liberation' and 'struggle', often used about the realization of a more just social order, are problematic. If we do not struggle against oppressive power, seeking to liberate other people from its exploitation and abuse, we fail in humanity and fellow feeling. If we do struggle against it, we inevitably give it substance and affirm its being by our very effort. One solution to this dilemma is to notice that all rigid, oppressive systems are run by fear in the oppressors and are constrained to operate in terms of a restricted grid of options. The oppressors seek to generate even more fear in the victims so that they too will conform to the same limited parameters of behaviour and social structure.

The transcendental solution to this has always been to lead people into the spaces the oppressive system does not command. In the old days these were physical, geographical spaces. Nowadays they are psychosocial and structural spaces. Rather than oppose abuse, create alternatives in spaces of this kind, spaces which the oppressors' fear makes it difficult for them to accept as existing. The trouble with struggle is that it may be in the grip of the fear induced by the oppressor, and so can act out that fear - at the highest level - in nonviolent confrontation, which affirms the power of the offensive system even while opposing it.

Once outside the hold of this fear, then the reformer has the open vision for innumerable options which the fear-ridden oppressor cannot see. Nonviolent reaction is replaced by creative proaction. Sometimes, of course, direct realization of some human right in a given situation is the same thing as challenging rigid social structures from without by direct nonviolent action. But the realization of the right is much more important than the challenge to the oppression.

The basic distinction here is between taking action to oppose abuses of human and planetary rights, and doing things which directly seek to fulfil those selfsame rights. (By planetary rights I mean the rights of all parts of the total planetary eco-system to be in mutually supportive balance with all other parts.) So we have opposition actions and fulfilment actions. Fulfilment actions may incidentally function as opposition actions but that is not their primary motive. Opposition *per se* has the potential problem of being fed by the compulsive and fixated rebellion of childhood. At its worst this means choosing targets that are too big and that result in repetitive ineffectiveness - a symbolic re-enactment of the fruitless struggles of the rebellious child.

Opposition *per se* also has the problem that the identity of the opposer becomes parasitic on the existence of the evil empire, and therefore supports it by needing it. The compulsive rebel is still dependent on the abuse of power which he or she struggles against, and is addicted to struggling with the fear which such abuse provokes. If, on the other hand, the prime end and reason for action is the fulfilment of human rights, rather than simply opposition to their abuse, then the agents concerned draw their identity from newly realized good rather than from the established bad, and will have more power and effect as a result.

Structural change options

Working on structural change at its own level has many forms, each of which is an arena for personal development and individual and collective action inquiry. In terms of the primary and secondary experiential learning cycles discussed in Chapter 3, the group members' endeavours in the world, their learning while doing, are the primary cycles; and these together with reflection and discussion on them at the group meetings are the secondary cycles.

The following groups may be created and sustained by a strong leader for a period, they may be facilitated on a rotating basis, they may run as peer groups on an agreed format. They all have to be conscious in the exercise of decision-making, finding a good balance between autonomy, co-operation and hierarchy. They will wisely be holistic in method and use the multi-stranded approach, incorporating elements from the several strands given at the end of Chapter 3.

1. Social change theory seminars. These are consciousness-raising study groups which research and reflect on the issues of change. Activism without this prior study can be blind, misplaced and ineffective. I have outlined three interrelated areas of theory - the psychosocial, the political-economic and the transpersonal. What seems critical is what these three approaches have to say to each other, and what active strategies such dialogue engenders. It makes sense for such seminars to use holistic methods which include: personal work on the emotional distress patterns that sustain addiction to oppressive systems both as victim and oppressor; a moral-political intellectual critique of the existing social order, interdependent with visions of a new society with first-step strategies that move toward it now, with both these wings backed up where possible by relevant research data; transpersonal attunement through the use of ritual, group resonance and inner unfoldment.

2. Community action groups. These are relatively small groups of people, variously affiliated by friendship, family, religion, social or occupational ties, who meet regularly to develop their ability to engage in some form of direct action for social change, in relation to any issue which is of concern to them. I repeat here the distinction made above between taking action to oppose abuses of human and planetary rights and doing things which seek to fulfil those selfsame rights and which, more generally, enable diverse forms of human flourishing. For the reasons stated, fulfilment actions seem preferable to opposition actions all on their own, and while the former may have a powerful impact as opposition actions that is not the reason for their execution. A community action group can include:

2.1. *Community development.* The group works directly, with or without the support of local government, to meet local needs and interests and deal with local issues, enlisting support and action from all those affected. This may involve social empowerment through consciousness-raising and appropriate action; revisioning and restructuring of their situation by oppressed minorities.

2.2. *Mutual aid.* The group sets up a mutual aid network within which people do work for each other on a reciprocal basis, in relation to an agreed range of tasks and an agreed system of exchange of labour.

2.3. *Peer self-help.* The group organizes a mutual support association whose members share a common need for experience sharing and succour. This may be in relation to a physical disability (congenital defect, later trauma, degenerative disease); social deviance (drug dependency, alcoholism, disabling social and psychological distress); life-crisis (divorce, separation, single parenthood, rape, physical violence, bereavement, redundancy, retirement); minority values (homosexual and lesbian life-styles, euthanasia, gender emancipation); personal development (co-counselling, peer Gestalt groups, etc); and so on.

2.4. *New society education.* The group is busy with raising its own and society's consciousness, with identifying relevant action, about cultural and ecological issues: overpopulation, green consumerism, consumer exploitation, recycling, pollution, abuse of the environment, animal rights, economic abuse of the third world, self-regulating eco-economics, soft technology and renewable energy, industrial democracy, work co-operatives, reduction of defence budgets.

3. Occupational action groups. These are groups that are affiliated exclusively by occupational ties: all the members of any group are from the same occupation, but not from the same organization or place of work (although some of them may be). Their commitment is to seek the extension and fulfilment of human and planetary rights within their own trade or profession and to create a climate for realizing more advanced views on psychological, social and political, ecological and transplanetary issues. They are likely to be active at professional conferences, meetings, committees, in-service training sessions, and so on. But initially they will be entirely *ad hoc* and not part of the formal structure of the profession.

4. Organizational action groups. These are groups of people who work together on the same organization. They may have the same occupational role, or they may be a mix of different occupations who work together. The commitment is to seek organizational change in the direction of increased self and peer determination of the sorts indicated in Chapter 5. The social structure is changed from within by political initiatives, persuasion, organizational development methods, and techniques of soft revolution. The aim is a better balance of hierarchy, co-operation and autonomy in the organization run as a learning centre. This sort of group will also initially be *ad hoc*, bringing its influence to bear informally through face-to-face dialogue, and also through formal organizational meetings of various kinds.

5. New institutions. All the previous activities converge on the creation of new institutions, the social structures of a new society. This seems a much wider arena for action than many people suppose, provided one is not in the grip of the fear which runs the prevailing system. Producers' and consumers' co-operatives, forms of community and village life which span the poles of privacy and communality, alternative schools, holistic medical clinics, these and many more require new skills in co-ownership, co-management and co-working: a challenge for any group of persons to live out a worthwhile way of life.

What need clarity are: the ability to work with distress feelings and not displace them on others; getting the right balance between autonomy and co-operation, and the allocation and rotation of hierarchical responsibility in well defined roles; the appropriate use of discussion methods and decision-making formats; awareness of group process issues; the institution as a learning and action inquiry centre going through cycles of experience and reflection, with intermittent study of related issues in the wider world; the availability of conflict resolution strategies; the use of supportive confrontation and questioning; the generation of new co-operative social practices; the grounding outlook of loving celebration and affirmation of people flourishing in their world; the creation of new rituals that deepen the meaning of shared living and working; openness to the subtle and spiritual dimensions of experience.

Facilitation for structural change

The facilitator as social change agent can take intitatives in setting up any one of the above groups, and can alert its members to the issues which they need to be aware of and take charge of if the group is to succeed. Some of these, including some of those just mentioned in the previous paragraph, are:

1. Emotion. The group members need to be able to separate out old hurts from present realities, and not to displace distress from the past into current agendas. It needs ways of working on distress that it stirred up by its actions in the world and its internal deliberations.

2. Power. The group needs to take charge of its way of making decisions. It needs to have a model of decision-making that is fully participative, consciously chosen and adhered to and systematically reviewed from time to time. It needs to rotate roles of facilitation, control and responsibility within the group on the basis of an honest assessment of competence and skill.

3. Inclusion. The groups needs to experiment with methods of discussion which ensure that everyone present has a voice and is heard. These methods can be reviewed and modified in the light of experience of them.

4. Gender. The group needs to be alert to the ways in which gender stereotypes can invade the behaviour and reactions of both men and women, and to have strategies for interrupting this and establishing enlightened gender relations.

5. Reflection. The group needs time to reflect on and learn from its actions in the world; and to study background material and reflect on that and its relevance to group goals and experience.

6. Co-operation. The group needs to replace the conventional norm of competition with one of co-operation, mutual aid and skill sharing.

7. Affirmation. The group needs to take time for its members to appreciate each other, their qualities and deeds and creations.

8. Celebration. The group needs time for rejoicing and festivity and fun.

9. Ritual. The group needs time to affirm its resonance with divine life and energy through shared ritual and contemplation.

10. Conflict. The group needs to have available strategies of conflict resolution and the awareness to use them when a conflict impasse is reached.

11. Confrontation. The group needs to be open to aware challenge and confrontation about its activities and assumptions by any one or more of its members, so that its does not get trapped in radical conformity and consensus collusion. The group also needs a climate in which it is possible for its members to give each other person-to-person negative feedback in a fundamentally supportive and respectful way.

At the frontiers of social change, those involved in any group of the kinds mentioned in this chapter are involved in collective action inquiry, whose primary cycles are embedded in intermittent secondary cycles, in both of which each person facilitates his or her peers in a mutuality of becoming.

References

Aitchison, J (1987) *Linguistics,* London: Hodder and Stoughton.

Alexander, F M (1969) *The Resurrection of the Body,* New York: Dell.

Allport, G (1958) 'The Historical Background of Modern Social Psychology', in Lindzey, G (ed), *Handbook of Social Psychology,* Cambridge, Mass.: Addison-Wesley.

Assagioli, R (1965) *Psychosynthesis,* Baltimore: Penguin Books.

Assagioli, R (1973) *The Act of Will,* New York: Viking Press.

Ausubel, D P (1960) 'The Use of Advance Organizers in the Learning of Meaningful Verbal Material', *Journal of Educational Psychology,* 51, 267-272.

Barlow, W (1973) *The Alexander Principle,* London: Gollancz.

Bateson, G (1979) *Mind and Nature,* London: Wildwood House.

Beardsley, M C (1958) *Aesthetics,* New York: Harcourt, Brace and World.

Boud, D (1988) 'Moving towards Autonomy', in Boud, D (ed), *Developing Student Autonomy in Learning,* London: Kogan Page.

Boud, D, Keogh, R and Walker, D (1985) 'Promoting Reflection in Learning: a Model', in Boud, D, Keogh, R and Walker, D (eds) *Reflection: Turning Experience into Learning,* London: Kogan Page.

Boud, D and Walker, D (1991) *Experience and Learning: Reflection at Work,* Geelong: Deakin University Press.

Boud, D and Walker, D (1992) 'In the Midst of Experience: Developing a Model to Aid Learners and Facilitators', in Mulligan, J and Griffin, C (eds) *Empowerment through Experiential Learning,* London: Kogan Page.

Brennan, R (1991) *The Alexander Technique,* Shaftesbury: Element.

Capra, F (1983) *The Turning Point,* London: Fontana.

Cortazzi, D and Roote, S (1975) *Illuminative Incident Analysis,* London: McGraw-Hill.

de Vries, M J (1981) *The Redemption of the Intangible in Medicine,* London: Institute of Psychosynthesis.

Egan, G (1990) *The Skilled Helper,* Pacific Grove, Calif: Brooks/Cole.

Flavell, J (1963) *The Developmental Psychology of Jean Piaget,* New York: Van Nostrand Reinhold.

Garratt, R (1987) *The Learning Organization,* London: Fontana.

Gerth, H H and Mills, C W (eds) (1984) *From Max Weber: Essays in Sociology,* London: Allen and Unwin.

Gowan, S, Lakey, G, Moyer, W and Taylor, R (1979) *Moving Toward a New Society,* Philadelphia: New Society Press.

Grof, S (1988) *The Adventure of Self-Discovery*, Albany: State University of New York Press.

Hadamard, J (1945) *The Psychology of Invention in the Mathematical Field*, New York: Dover Publications.

Handy, C (1985) *Gods of Management*, London: Pan Books.

Harrison, R (1972) 'Understanding Your Organization's Character', *Harvard Business Review*, May-June, pp 119-128.

Hawkins, P and Shohet, R (1989) *Supervision in the Helping Professions*, Milton Keynes: Open University Press.

Henry, J (1989) 'Meaning and Practice in Experiential Learning', in Weil, S W and McGill, I (eds), *Making Sense of Experiential Learning*, Buckingham: SRHE/Open University Press.

Heron, J (1977) *Behaviour Analysis in Education and Training*, Guildford: University of Surrey.

Heron, J (1979) *Co-counselling*, Guildford: University of Surrey.

Heron, J (1981a) 'Experiential Research Methodology', in Reason, P and Rowan, J (eds), *Human Inquiry*, Chichester: Wiley.

Heron, J (1981b) 'Philosophical Basis of a New Paradigm', in Reason, P and Rowan J (eds), *Human Inquiry*, Chichester: Wiley.

Heron, J (1982a) *Education of the Affect*, Guildford: University of Surrey.

Heron, J (1982b) 'Self and Peer Assessment for Managers', in Boydell, T and Pedler, M (eds), *Management Self Development*, Aldershot: Gower.

Heron, J (1985) 'The Role of Reflection in a Co-operative Inquiry', in Boud, D, Keogh, R and Walker, D (eds), *Reflection: Turning Experience into Learning*, London: Kogan Page.

Heron, J (1987) *Confessions of a Janus-Brain*, London: Endymion Press.

Heron, J (1988a) 'Assessment Revisited', in Boud, D (ed), *Developing Student Autonomy in Learning*, London: Kogan Page.

Heron, J (1988b) *Cosmic Psychology*, London: Endymion Press.

Heron, J (1989) *The Facilitators' Handbook*, London: Kogan Page.

Heron, J (1990) *Helping the Client: A Creative, Practical Guide*, London: Sage.

Heron, J (1992) *Feeling and Personhood: Psychology in Another Key*, London: Sage.

Hooper-Hansen, G (1992) 'Suggestopedia: A Way of Learning for the 21st Century', in Mulligan, J and Griffin, C (eds), *Empowerment through Experiential Learning*, London: Kogan Page.

Huczynski, A (1983) *Encyclopedia of Management Development Methods*, Aldershot: Gower.

Huxley, A (1963) *The Doors of Perception*, New York: Harper and Row.

Hyde, L (1955) *An Introduction to Organic Philosophy*, Reigate: Omega Press.

Jackins, H (1983) *The Reclaiming of Power*, Seattle: Rational Island Press.

James, W (1890) *The Principles of Psychology, Vols 1 and 2*, New York: Holt, Rinehart and Winston.

Jantsch, E (1980) *The Self-Organizing Universe,* Oxford: Pergamon.

Jung, C G (1977) *Psychological Types, Collected Works, Vol 6,* Princeton: Princeton University Press.

Kilty, J (1978) *Self and Peer Assessment,* Guildford: University of Surrey.

Kilty, J (1980) *Self and Peer Assessment and Peer Audit,* Guildford: University of Surrey.

Koestler, A (1964) *The Act of Creation,* London: Hutchinson.

Koestler, A (1978) *Janus,* London: Hutchinson.

Kolb, D A (1984) *Experiential Learning,* Englewood Cliffs, NJ: Prentice Hall.

Laszlo, E (1972) *Introduction to Systems Philosophy,* London: Gordon and Breach.

Lovelock, J (1987) 'Gaia: A Model for Planetary and Cellular Dynamics', in Thompson, W I (ed), *Gaia: A Way of Knowing,* Great Barrington, Mass: Lindisfarne Press,

Lozanov, G (1978) *Suggestology and Outlines of Suggestopedy,* New York: Gordon and Breach.

Maier, N R F, Solem, A R and Maier, A A (1975) *The Role Play Techniques,* Mansfield: University Associates of Europe Ltd.

Margulies, A (1984) 'Toward Empathy: The Uses of Wonder', *American Journal of Psychiatry,* 141, 1025-1033.

Miller, A (1987) *For Your Own Good: The Roots of Violence in Child-Raising,* London: Virago Press.

Mulligan, J (ed) (1988) *The Personal Management Handbook,* London: Sphere.

Mulligan, J and Griffin, C (eds) (1992) *Empowerment through Experiential Learning,* London: Kogan Page.

Nagel, E (1963) 'Wholes, Sums and Organic Unities', in Lerner, D (ed), *Parts and Wholes,* New York: Free Press of Glencoe.

Perry, R B (1954) *Realms of Value,* Cambridge, Mass: Harvard University Press.

Peters, R S (1966) *Ethics and Education,* London: Allen and Unwin.

Porritt, J and Winner, D (1988) *The Coming of the Greens,* London: Fontana.

Reason, P (1989) *Human Inquiry in Action,* London: Sage.

Reason, P and Heron, J (1986) 'Research with People', *Person-Centred Review,* 1, 4, pp 456-476.

Reason, P and Rowan, J (eds) (1981) *Human Inquiry: A Sourcebook of New Paradigm Research,* Chichester: Wiley.

Reid, T (1764) *Inquiry into the Human Mind on the Principles of Common Sense.*

Scheler, M (1954) *The Nature of Sympathy,* London: Routledge and Kegan Paul.

Schön, D (1983) *The Reflective Practitioner,* New York: Basic Books.

Schuster, D H and Gritton, C E (1986) *Suggestive Accelerative Learning Techniques,* New York: Gordon and Breach.

Swami Rama, Balletine, R and Swami Ajaya (1976) *Yoga and Psychotherapy,* Honesdale, Pa: Himalayan Institute.

Thame, S (1978) 'A Means of Understanding Human Learning; The Alexander Technique', *Management Education and Development*, 9, 3, pp 202-205.

Torbert, W (1991) *The Power of Balance: Transforming Self, Society and Scientific Inquiry*, Newbury Park, Calif: Sage.

von Bertalanffy, L (1972) *General Systems Theory*, London: Allen Lane.

von Eckartsberg, R (1981) 'Maps of the Mind: The Cartography of Consciousness', in Valle, R S and von Eckartsberg, R (eds), *The Metaphors of Consciousness*, New York: Plenum Press.

Weil, S W and McGill, I (eds) (1989) *Making Sense of Experiential Learning*, Buckingham: SRHE/Open University Press.

Wilber, K (1983) *Up from Eden*, London: Routledge and Kegan Paul.

Index